SOCIAL WORK ETHICS DAY TO DAY

Guidelines for Professional Practice

Carolyn Cressy Wells
   with
M. Kathleen Masch

WAVELAND
PRESS, INC.

Prospect Heights, Illinois

For information about this book, write or call:
Waveland Press, Inc.
P.O. Box 400
Prospect Heights, Illinois 60070
(708) 634-0081

TO MOM
who creates

Copyright © 1986 by Carolyn Cressy Wells and M. Kathleen Masch
1991 reissued by Waveland Press, Inc.

ISBN 0-88133-546-0

Printed in the United States of America

7

Contents

Foreword 1991

The opportunity to reissue *Social Work Ethics Day to Day* with Waveland Press, Inc. is a welcome one for me. While written in the mid-eighties, the book presents ethical issues frequently confronted in generalist social work practice today. The case examples took place in a particular agency setting ("Urban Day Center") during a particular period of time (the mid-1980s), so that the content will be left intact. To introduce new examples of ethical issues from the agency today, given various policy changes, would require a different book.

However, it may interest the reader to know that Urban Day Center remains alive and well in 1991. One important change has occurred which reflects the resolution of a problem presented in the book as an ethical dilemma: a half-day program is now available in addition to the full-time option. This policy not only provides more flexibility for determining appropriate intervention plans for particular children but allows more children to be served. Hence, while Urban Day continues to have four regular classrooms, (plus a new special care nursery serving 5 "medically fragile" infants, usually those of premature birth), 88 children may be served at any given time. Only 60 children could be served at one time during the mid-eighties. And since some children "graduate" to be succeeded by others, Urban Day actually served 131 children in the eleven-month period between November 1989 and September 1990, the most recent figures available for inclusion in this book.

In addition, expanded "outpatient" services are now available at Urban Day to children not enrolled in the regular full or half-day programs. These services (which may be arranged on a "private pay" basis) typically involve physical, occupational, or speech therapy.

Children served by Urban Day continue to be those with disabilities of various kinds. Enrollment in the full or half-day programs is limited to those children who exhibit 25% or greater delay in any two of five areas: motor skills (fine and gross), cognitive, self-help, socialization, and speech. A series of standardized tests and scales for scoring have been developed to measure delay. As in the mid-eighties, children are referred to Urban Day for evaluation by the Central Referral Committee of the county Combined Community Services Board. A welcome change is that children from all types of families are now referred to Urban Day, not just those from families perceived as abusive or neglectful. This policy resolves another ethical dilemma discussed in the book.

Children who are accepted for service in the full or half-day programs still receive all services free of charge. Most come from backgrounds of dire poverty. Of the 131 children served during the eleven-month period for which data was most recently available, 93 came from single-parent homes, 19 being born to mothers who were themselves only adolescents. Only 4 came from families including wage earners. All other children were dependent entirely on various types of public assistance, usually Aid to Families with Dependent Children or Supplemental Security Income. Seventy-seven children were born premature, perhaps due to the poor prenatal care common in circumstances of poverty.

Urban Day staff estimate that 20% of the children served by the agency today are victims of fetal alcohol syndrome, cocaine-affected or victims of other drug abuse. Official agency statistics do not reveal such a serious drug-related problem (3 referrals due to fetal alcohol syndrome, 9 cocaine-related, 7 "other drug"). But the diagnosis of 55 children accepted for service is simply "other," meaning uncertain. Staff believe many of these children have been impaired during fetal development due to drugs, because their symptoms resemble those of other children with positive drug-related diagnoses.

Staff has increased in some areas at Urban Day since this book was written, and decreased in others. Today the agency staff includes three social workers, five speech therapists, four occupational therapists, four physical therapists, one physical therapy aide, four teachers, and one registered nurse. The number of physical, occupational and speech therapists has increased due to the needs of the outpatient program. The social service staff has decreased by one member. However, all three of the social workers employed by the agency today have a BSW degree whereas, when the book was written, only the director had formal academic preparation. Academic training for the entire social work staff is certainly a change in the right direction. Undergraduate readers may be interested to know that the social service director today is a BSW (with supervisory experience prior to employment by Urban Day). She believes that the generalist perspective is crucial to competent performance of her work.

I would like to conclude by thanking Neil Rowe and Waveland Press, Inc. for the opportunity to reissue this book, and by thanking Cathy Arentsen for her assistance in updating information on Urban Day's clients, staff, and services.

Carolyn Cressy Wells

Preface

This is a book about ethics. More specifically, this is a book about social work ethics. In 1979 the Delegate Assembly of the National Association of Social Workers (NASW) revised the official code of this professional organization to reflect contemporary perspectives and experience. The NASW is the major national organization representing professional social workers in the United States today. It was formed in 1955 when several organizations of caseworkers, group workers, and community workers came together to form a national organization representing the social work profession as a whole. Membership is voluntary but requires at least a bachelor's degree in social work from a college or university program accredited by the Council on Social Work Education.

The Delegate Assembly of the NASW developed its first code of ethics in 1960 and amended this code in 1967 to include a provision requiring active elimination of discrimination against minorities. Since codes of ethics attempt to translate the values of a given profession into guidelines for correct professional behavior, it is understandable and appropriate that codes will change as the values and perspectives of the profession change. The NASW completely revised its professonal code of ethics in 1979, acting upon the recommendations of a special task force on ethics headed by Charles Levy.

In revising its code in 1979, the NASW provided practicing social workers with an important service. Social work practice decisions are often complex and involve choosing among a variety of imperfect options. Guidelines that can be applied to a variety of situations are needed. This is exactly what the revised social work code of ethics does—provide guidelines for ongoing practice decisions. The guidelines are based on and reflect long-held values of the social work profession, as well as new interpretations of these values.

The preamble states:

This code is based on fundamental values of the social work profession that include the worth, dignity, and uniqueness of all persons as well as their rights and opportunities. It is also based on the nature of social work, which fosters conditions that promote these values.

Given the social work professional values as stated in the preamble of the code, affirming the "worth, dignity, and uniqueness of all persons as well as their rights and opportunities," it is not surprising that the revised code of ethics emphasizes the social worker's accountability to clients. On the other hand, most social workers are employed in agencies sanctioned and financed by the public; consequently, they are also accountable to the public. Tension due to conflict between professional accountability to particular clients and to the public at large (usually as represented by the agency) is an ongoing reality in social work practice. The code takes a position emphasizing primary responsibility to clients, while also including distinct categories of principles relating to the social worker's ethical responsibilities to the agency, the profession, and society.

According to Elizabeth Howe (*Social Work,* May 1980), the individualistic model of practice provided by the revised code may be inappropriate for a "public" profession like social work. Howe also points out, however, that the code places strong emphasis on expansion of choice, which benefits not only individual clients but also society as a whole.

The social work code of ethics is a set of value-based guidelines for professional practice, as discussed above. Of course, no code can totally prescribe all practice behaviors. There are too many unique factors in each situation that must be taken into account. Hence the code comprises guidelines only, rather than a compilation of orders or prescriptions. These guidelines take the form of 16 practice principles, organized into six major categories. The individual social worker must be able to understand these principles well in order to consider their relevance in any given practice situation. The Preamble to the NASW Code of Ethics states:

In subscribing to and abiding by this code, the social worker is expected to view ethical responsibility in as inclusive a context as each situation demands and within which ethical judgment is required. The social worker is expected to take into consideration all the principles in this code that have a bearing upon any situation in which ethical judgment is to be exercised and professional intervention or conduct is planned. The course of action that the social worker chooses is expected to be consistent with the spirit as well as the letter of this code.

That is a tall order for an experienced practitioner, to say nothing of a beginner or a student. The preamble goes on to clarify that this is a major task.

In itself, this code does not represent a set of rules that will prescribe all the behaviors of social workers in all the complexities of professional life. Rather, it offers general principles to guide conduct, and the judicious appraisal of conduct, in situations that have ethical implications. It provides the basis for making judgments about ethical actions before and after they occur. Frequently, the particular situation determines the ethical principles that apply and the manner of their application. In such cases, not only the particular ethical principles are taken into immediate consideration, but also the entire code and its spirit. Specific applications of ethical principles must be judged within the context in which they are being considered.

The purpose of this book is to examine the social work code of ethics within the context of a particular agency's daily operations. Using a single agency's experience provides a model for decision making with which students can identify and compare their own practice issues and dilemmas. This book cannot prescribe practice behaviors any more than the code itself, but it can provide a variety of examples of how the principles of the code can be applied on a day-to-day basis.

The agency selected, an inner-city center for handicapped children, provides an excellent springboard for discussion and illustration of ethical issues in social work practice. The client population presents a variety of almost irreconcilable, irresolvable problems and needs, yet the social workers who work with the clients must make practice decisions all the time. In this particular setting the "ethical dilemma" discussion, generally more typical of the classroom, is ongoing, but the workers do not have the luxury of leaving issues unresolved. The social workers in the agency must act, usually on the basis of incomplete information, because real persons need assistance now. Thus the book illustrates not only ethical dilemmas as they arise but how social workers handle them. It also describes the end results for each practice example as far as is known. The book does not argue that the practice decisions described are perfect. Rather, the purpose is to demonstrate how decisions with ethical implications are made in one particular setting in this imperfect world. The process reveals the courage and integrity of social workers and clients alike in making their ongoing life choices, given the perceived options at hand.

The book also raises questions. It will become obvious to readers that the best interests of clients are not always clear. What society itself or the social work profession perceives as best may change with time, as, for example, in the case of Down's syndrome children. Institutionalization was once recommended for these children by most responsible professionals but is now considered the choice of last resort. Answers that seem correct today may appear wrong tomorrow. Social work professionals must continually consult to examine evolving concepts of ethical practice.

The social work code of ethics contains six major categories of principles. The book is organized so that each chapter after the introductory chapter examines one of these six categories. Each chapter begins with a statement of the particular major category of principles involved and then explores the related issues in practice. Case materials from the agency setting are offered to illustrate these issues and why they are problematic and significant. The major principles included under each category of the code are identified in subheadings and are also explored and illustrated with case examples from the agency setting.

This book is written primarily for students in social work, undergraduate or graduate. Courses for which this book would be most useful include methods courses, field instruction seminars, seminars in professional ethics, and other seminars or courses relating to social work as a profession and career.

Students in special education courses will also find this book useful, in helping to develop understanding of the variety of systems and stresses impinging on the children with whom they work.

The book is also intended to be useful for in-service training seminars for social service agency personnel. The case materials presented are concrete, easy to understand, and immediately applicable to decision making at the direct service level.

I wish to thank the people who helped me most with this book. Ron Federico helped me get started as both a social work educator and a writer. His encouragement, good humor, tact, and concrete suggestions helped me determine to complete the manuscript.

Irv Rockwood, my editor at the time I first submitted the manuscript, was instrumental in helping me clarify both purpose and prose. Later, David Estrin and Ronni Strell guided me through the final phases of development of the manuscript. I wish to express to all my sincere appreciation.

Kathleen Masch, my colleague in writing this book, deserves most of the credit for its birth. Although I did the actual writing, she provided the examples on which the writings are based. She reviewed each chapter as it was written and then critiqued the revisions. Her patience and energy continue to amaze me.

Of course, the staff of the agency presented here as "Urban Day Center" was crucial. Without the consent and cooperation of every member, this book could not have been developed.

Next, my family, especially my sister Merritt Stites, has shown sincere interest in my efforts and so has helped me sustain them.

Last, Elizabeth Schuman and her co-workers have demonstrated patience and skill in typing the manuscript, and Judith Roemer assisted me in preparing the supplementary readings section.

Carolyn Cressy Wells

1

Introducing the Agency Setting

The young woman sat staring down at the baby in her lap. She was slender and pretty. Her wavy brown hair fell gently over her shoulders, but her face looked haggard. In fact, her face had had a haggard look for several days, ever since her infant son, Don, was born.

Waves of fear and horror pulsed through her entire body, and she had to shake her head to clear it. This nightmare seemed to have been going on forever by now, and she couldn't keep herself from searching compulsively through her past, trying to figure out why this had happened to her. Mrs. Green felt as if she was being battered, severely punished for some reason, and this punishment was going to go on for the rest of her life.

"Well," she said in an almost inaudible voice, glancing up at the woman next to her, then lowering her eyes as she felt them fill with tears, "I guess I've had twenty-eight good years. Maybe that's all I can ask for."

She was flooded by new waves of feeling, this time guilt mixed in with the horror. Some people, after all, said that these things happened by God's will, and she had no right to question. The waves of anger and nausea she experienced from moment to moment were wrong. She should accept her fate.

As Mrs. Green's eyes fell back to her baby, the cause for the great pain so clearly present was not obvious. The baby boy looked healthy, and all four limbs were intact. But closer inspection revealed that his tongue protruded out of his mouth a little; the tongue looked thicker and larger than it should. The baby's eyes were odd in shape, a little wider in the middle than the average infant's eyes and slanted slightly upward.

Down's syndrome—that was the diagnosis made at birth by the doctor at the hospital. Down's syndrome meant that this baby, instead of having twenty-three pairs of chromosomes directing the development of his mind and body, had twenty-three pairs plus an extra. And for some reason still unknown, that forty-seventh chromosome has consistent and dreaded

1

results: Down's syndrome babies develop more slowly than other babies and grow up to be mentally retarded, never able to live entirely on their own, much less to provide for their elderly parents. Mental retardation is a foregone conclusion once the diagnosis of Down's syndrome is made, and there is no hope that the affected child will grow up to star on the soccer team, excel in school, or otherwise make the parents proud in the way most new parents dream. Neighbors and friends would call the child mongoloid and whisper about the tragedy.

The probability of conceiving a Down's syndrome baby is known to increase significantly after the age of thirty, so many mothers over thirty choose to undergo a test called amniocentesis to check for the condition. But Mrs. Green was only twenty-eight and had never been advised to have such a test. Nor would she have chosen to do so if advised, because of her youth and the fact that amniocentesis itself bears a slight risk to the pregnancy. A doctor must insert a needle into the mother's womb to draw out amniotic fluid, which can then be examined for chromosomal abnormalities. Mrs. Green had followed the best medical advice in carrying through with the most natural process of pregnancy possible and had been careful with her nutrition and her rest. But she had been very unlucky.

"I don't feel like God's chosen," Mrs. Green sobbed. "Why did this have to happen to me? Nobody's ever had a retarded child in my family before. Nobody understands. My parents are ashamed. I am ashamed. I know I shouldn't say this, but I don't want to be stuck with raising this child. For what?"

There was a time not so very long ago when most families who gave birth to Down's syndrome children would place them in institutions, private if they were wealthy and public if they weren't. That type of placement was considered ethical and responsible, a good example of how the concept of ethical behavior can change over time. The children would grow up among other handicapped children, spend their lives together, and die within the confines of the institution.

That usually spared their families a certain amount of pain and embarrassment, and in some cases, the institutions did provide the best possible care for the children. In some circumstances of severe handicap today, those involving severe mental retardation and physical deformity as well, institutional living may still be the best plan for a given child, at least among existing options. But gradually, beginning in the middle 1960s, an alternative philosophy or ethical perspective began to make its presence felt in this country. The alternative perspective can perhaps best be illustrated by its principle of the "least restrictive alternative." According to the principle of the least restrictive alternative, "handicapped" children, now relabeled "exceptional," can best be raised and educated in environments as close to normal as possible. The children can then have the best chance to enjoy life like other people, and even more, they can have people who are not handicapped around them on an ongoing basis to serve as role models. Children do, after all, learn a great deal through observation and play, and if they are observing and playing with normal people, they have the best chance to learn to behave normally themselves.

Many Down's syndrome children can learn to feed, dress, and toilet themselves, and to read and write at a simple level. Many seem to thrive on routine and thus can make patient, careful workers as adults, as long as their task is simple and repetitive. Down's syndrome adults can sometimes even hold a job and earn an income, though usually only in a specially designed "sheltered workshop" for handicapped people. They can live productive lives with only a little special supervision at work and at home. This is possible, though, only with an ongoing investment by parents and professionals of time, care, and skill. Caretaking and teaching roles with exceptional children are not easy, especially for the parents, who must wonder if the twenty-four-hour-per-day effort is worthwhile. As Mrs. Green agonized, for what? Certainly not for money, fame, achievement awards, or personal security, which are some of our society's major values. A clear answer for this question is not known, although many religious groups have produced explanations that work for some. Social work values asserting the worth and dignity of all persons provide an additional perspective. For others, the experience is simply a tragedy, requiring endless tedious work, and they run out of energy to deal with all the difficulties involved. How should they and Mrs. Green be helped?

URBAN DAY CENTER

Mrs. Green was sitting still and pensive, her Down's syndrome son, Don, in her lap, in the office of Mrs. Haley. Lauren Haley is a social worker, director of social services, at Urban Day Center, a treatment center for developmentally delayed children between birth and three years of age. Mrs. Green was referred to Urban Day Center by a special committee, the Central Referral Committee, which meets every month at the local children's hospital. This committee reviews the cases of community children with special needs who are brought to the attention of the committee by doctors, nurses, and social service personnel at the hospital, by public health nurses and social workers from all over the city, and by day-care center supervisors, ministers, and other community professionals who know of children believed to have special needs. Serving on the committee are doctors, nurses, social workers, speech therapists, and others qualified to make professional assessments of the children's needs and with knowledge of appropriate resources. The purpose of the committee is to refer the children to the community services that can best meet their needs.

Mrs. Green was referred to Urban Day Center by the Central Referral Committee because she lives in the geographic area served by the agency.

Moreover, her son needs all the services provided by Urban Day, and he needs them for a full day. He needs many services: the stimulation of teachers who are trained in early education methods for infants with developmental delays to maximize his educational potential; speech therapy because his enlarged tongue impedes normal speech development; occupational and physical therapy because Down's syndrome children tend to have problems with body coordination; and the services of a psychological consultant to identify major developmental delays in cognitive functioning and to measure progress.

The Green family also needs the close attention of the social service staff. It is the job of the social work staff to make sure each member of the treatment team knows how his or her work with the new baby, Don, coordinates with that of the others, and who makes sure that any special concerns of the family are communicated to the other staff members. Mrs. Green in particular needs the support of her social worker, Mrs. Haley, because Mrs. Green is so discouraged about her baby's retardation that she is about to give up on him. Without emotional support, Mrs. Green might just do that, which could result in a variety of even greater problems: possibly severe depression or an emotional breakdown, if Mrs. Green takes out her unhappiness on herself; or foster care or even institutionalization for Don if she continues to reject him. Worse, if Mrs. Green should decide she *wants* institutionalization for her son, she might not be able to obtain a placement for him because he would not be considered handicapped enough or because she could not afford the price of care. If foster care were not available either (foster families are scarce, especially those who will accept a retarded child), Don might have to live at home unwanted. A rejecting atmosphere with discouraged and ashamed adults can be as devastating for a young child as isolation or physical trauma. In terms of everyday behavior, rejection means that the child is not smiled at, talked to, held and cuddled, or played with very much, so that he or she does not receive sufficient stimulation for proper development. Teachers at Urban Day, as well as social service staff, provide an important source of support for struggling parents. However, they seldom have the opportunity to give that role so much professional thought and attention, or to make home visits for this purpose. They spend most of their working day within their classrooms, attending to the simultaneous needs of approximately sixteen children.

Mrs. Haley sat next to Mrs. Green, listening carefully to her and observing little Don as he drooled on his mother's lap. "It must be really tough for her," she thought. "It's easier for the people who feel as if they have been chosen in some way to have a special child. But Mrs. Green feels that she's been slapped and she doesn't know why." And as Mrs. Haley and Mrs. Green looked down at the little boy with Down's syndrome, he opened his eyes and burped loudly. Then he spat up his breakfast, all over his mother's right leg. Don wasn't even cute, actually, not even by a generous stretch of the imagination. He was large and rather homely, as babies go. Mrs. Green's jaw set hard as if willing herself to endure.

Mrs. Haley thought to herself how in each situation of working with a person or family with a handicapped child, she was a social worker and a human being at the same time. Her formal role was to provide support, information, and coordination of services. She was a professional to whom Mrs. Green could speak her feelings openly and honestly, and so have a chance to know, examine, and thus have the potential to rework them. There would be no right or wrong feelings in Mrs. Haley's office: just feelings, intense feelings, and a lot of them. By laying these intense feelings out in a safe place of acceptance and understanding, Mrs. Green would gradually be able to understand and accept herself, and so the energy she was channeling into guilt and shame could be rechanneled toward creating new meaning for her particular life. Formally, Mrs. Haley was a professional whose purpose was to help Mrs. Green solve her problems. In addition, Mrs. Haley knew she felt a personal commitment to the Green family. She wanted to make a significant difference to the young couple and their baby, so that their lives might feel worth living again. Or else she would not be in this line of work. Together, she affirmed to herself, we're going to find something here.

And Mrs. Haley began to talk with Mrs. Green.

BACKGROUND INFORMATION

Urban Day Center is not the real name of the agency described in this book. The names, places, and certain other characteristics of both the agency and the people and their circumstances have been changed to protect the privacy of the real people whose stories appear here. The center is an inner-city agency. Let us call the city Project City, not its real name, of course. It is located somewhere in midwestern United States. Mrs. Green, who has a middle-class background, professional occupational status, and an intact marriage is in fact an unusual client for this agency. Most of the clients at Urban Day are poor, unemployed, and of minority ethnic status, very much like most of the people in the neighborhood where the agency is located. The agency was founded only in the late 1960s, in response to a very real need in Project City for a program that would provide early stimulation and education for handicapped children, particularly for children from poor and culturally deprived families.

To describe the clientele of Urban Day in more detail, the agency serves sixty children, aged three or under. Over half of the children enrolled are black, about a quarter are white, and the rest represent a variety of other ethnic backgrounds. The reason that the children receive services at the center only until they are three is because the public school system is required by law to provide early education services for children with special needs who are aged three or older. Urban Day is therefore not eligible for any public funding for services to children older than three.

More than sixty infants and toddlers are actually served in a given calendar year at Urban Day, because as some leave, others take their places. In 1982, for example, the total enrollment was 101. Fifty-six percent were male, 44 percent female. Sixty-three percent were black, 23 percent white, 9 percent Hispanic, 1 percent Oriental, 1 percent Native American, and 3 percent "other." Ninety-eight percent of all children served were developmentally delayed, intellectually or physically. Eighty-five percent had physical impairments, including vision problems (14 percent), hearing difficulties (15 percent), cerebral palsy or suspected cerebral palsy (25 percent), and genetic impairments (17 percent). Many had obvious but as yet undiagnosed physical problems. Several had symptoms associated with fetal alcohol syndrome. Twenty-nine percent were mentally retarded, and another 3 percent were diagnosed as emotionally disturbed. About 80 percent were considered high-risk children, that is, children from families who couldn't take care of them very well. Because of problems on the part of the parents, the children were likely to suffer from lack of stimulation at home or perhaps even from physical abuse. The most serious cases like these were usually referred by Blue County Protective Services and accounted for fully 36 percent of the children at the center.

Most of the children served by Urban Day in 1982 were also very poor. Eighty-five percent came from families who were dependent on public welfare, and 91 percent received medical assistance moneys from Title XIX of the Social Security Act which is available only to families poor enough to meet a very severe means test. Seventy-eight percent of the children came from single-parent families, and 15 percent had adolescent mothers.

The formal organizational structure of Urban Day is illustrated on page 7. As can be seen from the organizational chart, this private, nonprofit agency is governed by a board of directors, which establishes agency policy. The executive director translates board policy into the day-to-day rules and regulations that govern the agency's operations. Under the executive director is the program director, who is responsible for coordinating the operation of the various agency departments: education, social services, therapy (physical, occupational, and speech), medical (which includes the dietician and the maintenance staff at Urban Day), volunteer, and clerical.

In circumstances like Urban Day's where such a large percentage of the client population comes from highly deprived circumstances, a strong social service staff is very important in assessing underlying needs and connecting needy families with potential resources. Urban Day employs a social service staff of four. The director or supervisor, Mrs. Haley, has a master's degree in social work and in fact did her graduate school field

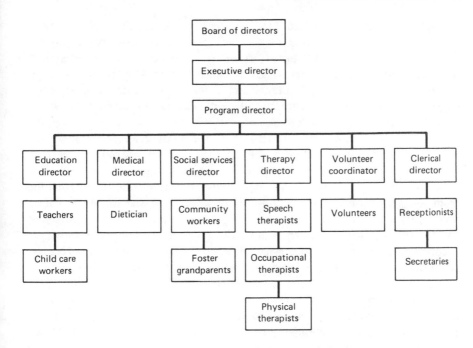

placement at Urban Day. When she accepted the job, she was already well prepared to meet the needs of the agency. The three members of her staff who work under her, called community workers at Urban Day, earned their current positions by previously doing effective work in other positions at the agency. This occurred during the early 1970s. At this time it was accepted or even preferred to hire social service staff from among the grass roots, or people who understand the needs of the client population through personal or work experience but who do not have the educational degrees normally required to achieve such positions. These workers have stayed with Urban Day. Mrs. Haley maintains open communication with the staff under her supervision so as to teach and maintain high standards of service. The social service department at Urban Day is known for its willingness to take on the often thankless task of tracking down every child referred, and for its persistent work with parents in order to give each referred child the best possible chance to receive the specialized services available at the agency.

Urban Day also employs on a regular basis four teachers, sixteen child-care workers who work in the classroom and play areas with the teachers, three speech therapists, two physical therapists, and two occupational therapists. All of the children are worked with by the teachers and child-care workers; in 1982, 88 percent also received special services from the speech therapists, 74 percent from the occupational therapists, and 79 percent from the physical therapists. Special tests are required to determine eligibility for these services. Many of these are given by the respective therapists themselves. Urban Day also maintains ongoing relationships with a number of consulting physicians, and a consulting psychologist, psychiatrist, and even a dentist in order to conduct other tests and measurements as needed for a given child. Urban Day performs as a training agency as well; students in social work, education, speech, physical and occupational therapy all gain intensive in-service education with the various departments.

A delightful aspect of Urban Day is the variety and energy of the volunteers it attracts. Because the children served are so young and appealing, many volunteers spend their time at the agency helping with a wide variety of child care tasks. Approximately fifty volunteers, ranging from suburban housewives to high school students, assist the staff. These volunteers are recruited and scheduled by a full-time volunteer coordinator. In addition, the agency maintains a foster grandparent program which is coordinated by the social services director. Foster grandparents receive some monetary reward for their services and must meet a certain income requirement in order to be eligible. However, like all other volunteers, their primary reward is the relationship with the children and sense of contributing to the growth and development of young human beings. Foster grandparents each have one or two children who are primarily theirs to nurture and motivate.

According to carefully recorded agency statistics, Urban Day produces more service units at less cost than any other agency in Project City that works with developmentally delayed children. This does not mean, however, that Urban Day's excellent record is always rewarded. When funds are adequate, Urban Day receives more referrals than it can handle. But lately funds have not been adequate. As a result, children are being sent by the Central Referral Committee to agencies providing half-day services. Until recently they would have sent these same children to Urban Day's full-day program. Per unit of service cost at Urban Day is a bargain, but if a child receives services all day long, the total cost of the services is higher than the total cost of the more expensive half-day services. Today, public-sector social service funds are increasingly scarce in this country as the various levels of government struggle to balance the budget while, at the federal level, the military runs up the largest deficits ever known to the nation.

Referrals to the half-day agencies save dollars now in the interest of budget cuts but will probably be more expensive in the long run. These agencies, at least in Project City, do not have strong social service staffs, so many referred children are simply not served at all. There is no one with the responsibility or time to follow up on referrals when parents do not bring in their children. These agencies currently do not have the time or the philosophy to chase down initially unmotivated parents, simply postponing to the future the cost that society will someday have to pay to service the people who, through lack of early intervention when they were children, became permanently handicapped adults. Moreover, many of the children who are brought in for early intervention and treatment in Project City simply need more attention than the half-day programs can offer them.

Urban Day's funds are provided by the following sources: Combined Community Services Board of Blue County, 55 percent; United Way, 10 percent; Title I (Public Law 89–313), 8 percent; Title XIX of the Social Security Act (Medicaid), 20 percent; United States Department of Agriculture (for food supplies), 2 percent; and various private grants, 5 percent. Funds are presently adequate but since the County Combined Community Services Board is becoming increasingly reluctant to approve any child for full-day funding, regardless of need, the agency may have to change its program to half-day and is currently considering doing so.

HIGH RISK AND ITS RELATIONSHIP TO HANDICAP

Some of the handicapped children served by Urban Day are actually born handicapped —with precisely diagnosable difficulties like Down's syndrome, spina bifida, microcephaly, hydrocephaly, and cerebral palsy. Some are born with clearly visible physical deformities, yet a diagnosis is elusive. And some are born normal physically and mentally in every way but are victims of another kind of bad luck. They are born into profoundly troubled family situations. Their mother may be a single parent who lacks the time or emotional stability to pay attention to a child. One or both parents may be developmentally delayed themselves, perhaps even mildly retarded. In other situations the mother is exceptionally young, in the middle or early teens. In these situations, children who are normal at birth can become developmentally delayed because of lack of appropriate stimulation. Without assistance from the outside, the delay becomes permanent. Such problems don't lie with the children but rather with the parents and an unsupportive society. With early intervention, these children can develop normally.

Society's feelings about helping these children are often mixed, and that is the reason Urban Day provides an unusual service. The agency provides preventive programming to children in high-risk family situations as well as to children born with physical handicaps. This is rare in the United States. That isn't because society consciously blames babies for their misfortune at being born into disadvantaged families and thus refuses to intervene in their behalf. But society *does* blame the parents. According to our dominant cultural values, parents should provide for their children. This appears to be a fine value. But often parents can't provide adequately for their children, because the parents are developmentally delayed and/or deprived themsleves. Perhaps neither the parents' parents nor society provided appropriate stimulation for them either, so they became delayed in childhood and the situation atrophied permanently. When they reached childbearing age, then, they were unable to carry out normal parental tasks properly. Society then blames them as adults for their inadequacy, and the discouraging game continues.

Before Urban Day Center was founded, most of the already handicapped or high-risk children in Project City went without special care. By the time they reached school age, they were already hopelessly delayed. Urban Day Center was organized to give these children a chance.

From Urban Day's conception, social services were built into the structure of the agency, and that is one reason this agency was selected as the subject of this book. The founders of the agency were social workers. Social work as a profession endeavors to enhance the social functioning of all people and promotes the development of environmental conditions that will help people achieve their maximum potential. Thus social workers work with individuals, families, groups, organizations, and communities to help improve the quality of life for all.

The founders of Urban Day realized that in order to meet the needs of the variety of handicapped children who lived in Project City, they would have to develop a new agency or program. So they utilized their social work skills in community work and organizational planning and developed an agency that would work with handicapped children primarily as special individuals.

However, the founders also understood that it wouldn't be just the children who would be the clients at Urban Day. As in the case of Mrs. Green, many parents also would need help to confront and deal with their feelings regarding the birth and rearing of a child viewed as imperfect. Other parents would be so handicapped themselves, because of their own early deprivation and related emotional and intellectual disturbance, that they would be unable to get their children to the agency for the specialized services available there. Some parents would feel so defeated by their own experiences in life that they really wouldn't care whether their children got help or not. Others might care but would be unable to get up in the morning to get their children to school, because of depression, alcoholism, bad habits, or some other reason. These parents would require daily prodding by social service staff.

Some parents would fear the professional appearance of the agency itself and be too shy to enter the building without personal encouragement. Some parents wouldn't believe the school could help their children, and they would require intensive outreach before becoming willing to give their permission for their child to receive services. Some would be willing to put their children on the bus to school in the morning but would not be willing to take part in what was happening to their children at Urban Day. From Urban Day's point of view this situation would be preferable to the parents' neglecting to send their children at all, but this pattern of parental behavior would present a different problem. When the children attained the age of three and left the agency, they might have achieved normal skills for their age level. Thus they would be ineligible for special education services from the public schools, yet the parents would not be able to carry on Urban Day's work at home to maintain normal behavior. Most of what Urban Day gave to the child could then be lost due to apathy or ignorance on the part of the parents. Like it or not, work with the parents would have to be an integral part of Urban Day's services or what Urban Day accomplished with the children would be undone.

Another reason this agency was chosen to be the subject of this book has to do with the variety of ethical issues constantly arising at the agency. What about the social work principle of self-determination, in a situation where a culturally deprived, hostile young parent does not want to bother to get his or her child ready for school in the morning? What about keeping a place open for a child at the agency even though the parent doesn't send him or her, except on rare occasions, because of morning hangovers? The social service staff knows that if the agency gives up on this family, no other will take up the challenge. And yet, if a place is to be kept open at Urban Day for the child, another needy infant may have to remain on the waiting list for service. How does one get parents more involved in the everyday workings of the center without annoying more task- and case-oriented professional staff, who may feel that the parents get in the way? And how does one maintain confidentiality when parents frequently interact with each other at the agency and then want to find out from the social worker what another parent, who hasn't been around lately, is doing about some particular problem? These are just a few of the specific ethical dilemmas that will be discussed in this book.

To summarize, Urban Day Center is a small inner-city agency providing early education and therapy for very young children who have a variety of developmental problems. The children served are three or under because beginning at the age of three, the public schools are mandated to serve children with developmental delays. Most of the parents of the children enrolled at Urban Day have a variety of problems themselves, sometimes so severe that they cannot even understand that the agency can help their children. And Urban Day *must* reach the children through these parents because legally, parents must agree in writing to accept the services of the agency, or the children cannot receive them. Of course some parents, convicted of child neglect or abuse, have been ordered by the court to enroll their children at the agency. In general, these parents are initially hostile and resistant; their feelings and fears can powerfully affect further development of the children involved. In short, Urban Day's task of serving handicapped children, particularly the many multiproblem handicapped children that are so tragically common in inner-city neighborhoods, is a tremendously difficult one. The agency is willing to accept children that no other agency can take on, even children whose parents have to be led to the agency by the hand before they will permit their children to be enrolled. In many ways, Urban Day is an agency of last resort; it serves the clients no one else wants.

REVIEW

The preface of this book introduces the social work code of ethics, as revised by the National Association of Social Workers in 1979. Chapter 1 describes Urban Day Center and the nature of its work. Examples from current social work practice at Urban Day will be used throughout the book to help illustrate the meanings of the various principles of the social work code of ethics.

The content of the code is organized according to the following six major headings: (1) The Social Worker's Conduct and Comportment as a Social Worker, (2) The Social Worker's Ethical Responsibility to Clients, (3) The Social Worker's Ethical Responsibility to Colleagues, (4) The Social Worker's Ethical Responsibility to Employers and Employing Organizations, (5) The Social Worker's Ethical Responsibility to the Social Work Profession, and (6), The Social Worker's Ethical Responsibility to Society. In each of the remaining chapters of this book, one of the six major categories of principles will be illustrated and discussed in detail. For your convenience, the entire code is reprinted in the Appendix at the end of this book.

STUDY QUESTIONS

1   For what reasons does a profession like social work need a code of ethics? How can a code of ethics be useful to social work practitioners?

2   Does the NASW code of ethics present social workers with a set of rules that will prescribe practice decisions? Why or why not?

3   Since the code of ethics, as revised in 1979, appears useful and relevant for social workers today, do you expect that it will remain as is in the distant future? Why or why not?

4   How and why was Urban Day founded? Why was a social service staff built into the organizational structure of the agency when the agency's primary purpose is to provide education and physical, occupational, and speech therapy to handicapped children?

5   What are the basic characteristics of most of the children served by Urban Day in terms of ethnic heritage and socioeconomic class?

6   Why was Urban Day selected as a useful agency to help illustrate the application of the principles of the code of ethics to decision making in daily social work practice?

2

The Social Worker's Conduct and Comportment as a Social Worker

Mrs. Dillon sat hunched over the telephone, clenching her palms and fingers into two tight fists, frustrated. Mrs. Dillon, an energetic, attractive black woman, one of the community workers on Mrs. Haley's social service staff, was in the middle of a phone conversation with Ms. Johnston, a single, twenty-one-year-old black mother of two. Both of Ms. Johnston's children were enrolled at Urban Day. Or rather, they were supposed to be enrolled at Urban Day. For the hundredth time, it seemed, Mrs. Dillon was politely discussing with Ms. Johnston why the children weren't at school that day. The youngest, little Bobbie, one year and seven months of age, had been referred by the cerebral palsy clinic at Project City Children's Hospital only two months before.

Mrs. Dillon had scheduled a routine intake evaluation for Bobbie, upon request of the hospital clinic worker. During an intake evaluation a parent brings a referred child to Urban Day, and the staff conducts a variety of tests to find out if the child actually needs Urban Day's services. The classroom teacher and the physical, occupational, and speech therapists all observe the child and discuss behavior at home with the parent. This initial evaluation is scheduled and coordinated by the social services staff, hence Mrs. Dillon's personal contact with Ms. Johnston.

Mrs. Dillon had found out during the first telephone conversation that Ms. Johnston didn't have a car. The mother had said she would need transportation to bring her child in to the center. Mrs. Dillon was not able to pick the mother up at the time available for the intake because of other case responsibilities, but she checked with her supervisor, Mrs. Haley, and found that Mrs. Haley could transport the young mother.

When Mrs. Haley went to get Ms. Johnston and her son Bobbie, she found not only one child in the home who had cerebral palsy, but two. There was an older sister, Luann, two years and seven months of age, sitting like Bobbie in a large playpen. Mrs. Haley was glad to find that the house where the family lived was fairly clean and neat, because that was a good indication that this mother might be organized and able to care for her children.

Both Bobbie and Luann demonstrated the jerky movements of cerebral palsy children and showed severe contractures of their limbs from the combined factors of the physical condition they were born with and from insufficient movement and exercise since birth. Mrs. Haley felt that both children needed special services, and so she decided to bring them both to Urban Day for evaluation. But even though her trip to Ms. Johnston's home had been scheduled in advance, Ms. Johnston now told Mrs. Haley that she wasn't ready to come in. The social service director had to go back to Urban Day without her two potential clients.

Later that day, Ms. Johnston did bring both children in to Urban Day with the aid of a neighbor. At the urgent request of Mrs. Haley, the rest of the Urban Day staff juggled their schedules so they could do an initial evaluation that day. Both children were found eligible for service because of the physical contractures of their limbs, their stiff and uncoordinated bodies, and, as best as could be determined from the initial evaluation of behavioral skills, mental retardation. In addition, Bobbie's eyes were severely crossed and he seemed to be suffering from an asthma-like condition.

The children, however, missed the bus on the first day they were supposed to go to school. Their mother didn't have them ready on time. Mrs. Dillon went to the home to collect the children herself. This unfortunate behavior continued. On the phone, the young mother's voice had a defensive, "don't bother me" quality. Though her children had been formally enrolled at Urban Day for seven weeks, the mother had failed to put them on the bus eight of the days. Mrs. Dillon had gone to pick up the children for five of the days. On one of the days Ms. Johnston had said the children were sick, so they stayed home. For two of the days the family was out of town, according to the person who answered the phone. Then the family moved and the mother neglected to inform Urban Day, so the bus did not go to the right address to get the children. The day preceding the phone call, Mrs. Dillon had finally located the children again through the maternal grandmother and she had gone to the family's new apartment to bring the children to school herself.

Once Mrs. Dillon had straightened out the address matter with Ms. Johnston and the bus company, she had hoped the mother would send her two children to school regularly. But she didn't. Attendance seemed to be deteriorating, a bad omen. Mrs. Dillon scheduled a home visit with Ms. Johnston, this time not only to pick the children up but to discuss attendance as a serious issue. She also hoped to get Ms. Johnston's signature on special forms for the Project City Special Education Program so that little Luann, two years and nine months of age by now, could be evaluated for service by the public schools. Once Luann attained the age of three, she would no longer be eligible for funding at Urban Day. If she were to receive more special education services, she would have to be enrolled in the public school programs for preschool handicapped children.

It is this sort of particular practice situation to which the more general principles of the social work code of ethics must be applied. In this chapter, the focus will be on important practice implications of the first major principle of the code, the social worker's conduct and comportment as a social worker. Each chapter that follows focuses on one of the five remaining categories of principles.

The social worker's conduct and comportment refer to how the social worker behaves or acts. More specifically, this portion of the code addresses the ethical component of the practitioner's professional behavior *as a social worker*. It includes five specific principles concerning propriety; competence and professional development; service; integrity; and scholarship and research. Each of the principles thus identified as fundamental to the social worker's conduct and comportment will be examined in this chapter, but in order to provide a context for application, let us return to the Johnston family.

WORKING WITH DEPRIVED FAMILIES

In the case of the Johnston family, staff concern about the children's poor attendance was rising. When the children did attend the center, Bobbie in particular showed a growing interest in trying to move himself around. In his classroom at Urban Day he would drag-crawl himself along by pulling with his arms and hauling his legs. He butted people hard with his head if they happened to get in his way as he pulled himself along, and he could leave impressive bruises on unprotected shinbones. People learned to move out of his line of direction when they got to know him better! But the staff at Urban Day encouraged Bobbie to move, even though it certainly was a bit inconvenient at times, and he was growing more and more able to do so. The physical therapist worked with him daily to help reduce the contractures of his arms and legs; the speech therapist encouraged him to make sounds so that he could begin to make contact with his environment other than by butting into it. With all this specialized attention, Bobbie was, for the first time, being given the chance to develop into an aware and functioning person, even though his physical mobility would always be limited. The staff began to realize that, intellectually, Bobbie was probably normal. A child as severely disabled physically as

Bobbie could not respond normally to an IQ test when first evaluated by Urban Day, even one for young children. He could not answer questions by pointing to things, by nodding his head, by saying simple words. So both Bobbie and Luann tested out utterly retarded at first. But soon Bobbie was gaining some motor control; he could use a simple pointer in response to questions, and had some limited use of speech, which could be aided by correct body positioning. Bobbie's responses to questions and directions were beginning to suggest that he was probably normal in terms of his mental abilities. He could respond appropriately to the teacher's words, smiles, gestures, and eye contact, even if only in his own particular way so limited by his tight and twisted body. He had formed a close emotional bond with one of the child-care workers and seemed to work especially well for her.

But without Urban Day's intervention, both Bobbie and Luann would spend most of their time in a crib or playpen at home, becoming more and more stiff and twisted. So the staff cared whether they got to the center each day. It was the task of the social service workers to influence the mother, Ms. Johnston, to get the children to the agency on a regular basis. And the cooperation of Ms. Johnston, marginal from the beginning, was deteriorating.

The Johnston case, which is not atypical of work with a deprived, multiproblem family, helps illustrate why not everyone is cut out for social work. The stereotypical bleeding-heart type that fables say goes into the field wouldn't make it past the first week in a situation like this. Ms. Johnston's lack of awareness of all the trouble to which the staff at Urban Day goes would not make a do-gooder radiate with well-being. The hoped-for reward of gratitude in return for good works is simply absent. Ms. Johnston is unaware of the good works as often as she notices them, and at times she actually seems to resent the opportunities presented because they do not fit in with her priorities.

And what Urban Day has to offer does *not* fit her priorities. Ms. Johnston has herself been raised in the inner city. Her surroundings for her entire life have been dingy and depressing. Raised in a poor family, she has not had much to be proud of in her life. She has owned few good clothes and almost no other personal property except dime-store jewelry. Due to the poverty of her parents, her diet has been marginal throughout her life. Her emotional stability has, in all probability, been affected by her poor nutrition as has that of many of her family and friends. She lives in an environment where it is necessary to be constantly on guard or the few possessions she owns will be stolen. For this reason she, like her neighbors, keeps her curtains pulled shut twenty-four hours per day so that no one interested in theft can see inside her apartment to locate the meager belongings within. This measure protects her safety to some degree but insures that her drab apartment will feel habitually damp and dark, as well as isolated. As can be imagined, the overall atmosphere within the home is depressing. At twenty-one years of age Ms. Johnston has the responsibility of two crippled children to raise alone, and she has no high school diploma and no job in an age of high unemployment. Her present life is bleak, her future prospects even bleaker. In short, she has no hope of obtaining things she has never experienced. Her tendency is to try to escape her difficult reality as best she can. Financially unable to pick up and leave the inner city, she takes the way out most readily offered by her social environment—alcohol and drugs. Chemical substances can help for the moment, and they can help quickly. They are available to the have-nots in the inner city.

So sometimes, in fact often, Ms. Johnston tries to escape her reality and relieve her emotional depression by drinking. When Urban Day contacts her about providing services for her children, she doesn't really pay much attention. She certainly doesn't expect genuine help from the agency, because her life experiences haven't prepared her to expect such things. Besides, she isn't sure she wants her children away from her during the day. In her empty life, sometimes even her crippled children provide welcome company during the day, and sometimes her mother drops by to see them.

Ms. Johnston doesn't respond to Urban Day's initial outreach, then, because she doesn't expect very much and doesn't think she wants the services anyway. She doesn't have her children ready to go for evaluation on the day of her first scheduled appointment to tour the center for two major reasons. She doesn't believe agency staff will really come to transport her, and she wants to check out any staff if they do come to her home. Both reasons can be viewed as valid and natural from her perspective. In a sense, Ms. Johnston's decision to bring Bobbie and Luann into the center for evaluation herself after meeting Mrs. Haley was a testimonial to the competent work of the social service director. Ms. Johnston obviously felt safe with Mrs. Haley and was therefore motivated to check out Urban Day. Of course, she didn't realize at this time that the agency staff were hightly inconvenienced by her unscheduled appearance late in the working day. She didn't know that many staff members changed their schedules and left ongoing work to test Bobbie and Luann. Furthermore, had the Urban Day staff acted out any sense of annoyance or inconvenience due to her late unexpected visit, Ms. Johnston would have been frightened away again, probably for good.

But the Urban Day staff treated Ms. Johnston with respect. Ms. Johnston's confidence was won and she voluntarily signed the necessary papers giving permission for service. The poor attendance of the children beginning almost immediately and then getting worse was due to something besides fear and disbelief in the Urban Day program. Other factors were involved that needed to be investigated. It would be the job of the social service staff to determine the underlying problems that were keeping Ms. Johnston from making use of Urban Day's program. On the surface, it seems so obvious that a mother should be grateful to have such a resource to turn to.

Confronted with a situation like this, an untrained worker might explode with irritation and drop the family from the caseload as unworthy and unmotivated. The family, in turn, would obligingly refrain from requesting further service. In fact, agencies without a social service staff would probably never have begun to work with this family in the first place. Instead, when Ms. Johnson said she could not get to the agency due to lack of a car, she would have been told to call back when she could find transportation. Naturally she wouldn't have called. Nervousness about what she was getting into, or disbelief that there was anything worthwhile out there, would have led her to drop the entire matter.

Maintaining the energy and ability to work with multiproblem, apparently unmotivated parents involves professional perspectives and expertise. The untrained lay person, even the kindly, caring lay person, would perceive Ms. Johnston to be irresponsible and undeserving, and soon the result of such a perception would be a loss of interest in working with her.

From the perspective of the professional social worker, however, Ms. Johnston can be viewed as a member of a deprived and depriving environment. Simply blaming her for her inadequate parenting and dropping her from the caseload because she seems unmotivated and ungrateful are not useful responses to her behavior. Dropping her case not only contributes to further deprivation for her, but abandons her children who cannot be blamed for anything at this time in their young lives. Ms. Johnston's erratic and self-defeating behavior, while difficult to work with, can be understood as a relatively unsurprising reaction under the circumstances, rather than as intentionally provocative or ungrateful. After all, at age twenty-one she is the mother of two handicapped children without a partner to ease her burden. She is also living below the poverty level on public welfare with children who have exceptional needs, a situation that could daunt a woman from the most privileged of backgrounds.

COMPETENCE AND PROFESSIONAL DEVELOPMENT

The first category of principles of the code of ethics is "The Social Worker's Conduct and Comportment as a Social Worker," which is the major focus of this chapter. The first major principle in this category, propriety, will be discussed later. We shall first deal with the second principle, competence and professional development, because it relates so clearly and immediately to the Johnston case.

Many people think they would like to become social workers because they like to help people and enjoy confiding in others or having others confide in them. There is no reason why people who like people wouldn't make good social workers. In fact, this characteristic is probably a necessary ingredient for a good practitioner. However, liking to help people is not sufficient to make a good social worker. This characteristic must be augmented with careful study by the prospective worker, both academic and in the field, including carefully monitored practice experience supervised by qualified social workers. The reasons are many, but perhaps the simplest, as suggested by the Johnston case, is that many social work clients provide their workers with few if any of the expected rewards for service. Clients who should be open, confiding, and grateful for assistance often aren't—and often with good reason. The untrained worker, however, remains unaware of the reasons and ultimately feels like a failure, very angry, or even ill-used and burned-out. The sad result is the waste of a potentially fine social worker and a client or set of clients whose underlying needs haven't even been perceived, much less met. In the case of Bobbie and Luann Johnston, for example, the presenting problem is cerebral palsy, and that can be perceived easily by lay person and professional alike. But the underlying social, psychological, and economic needs of both children and mother will be understood only through a careful, informed process of problem assessment.

It is difficult enough for an educationally qualified, experienced social worker to keep working with multiproblem clients given the stacked odds against any kind of successful problem resolution. However, educated and experienced workers are more likely to be able to endure because: (1) they are educated to initiate a careful process of problem assessment and to avoid jumping to conclusions; (2) they are less likely to expect immediate success; (3) they are less likely to simply blame the victim for what is going wrong; and (4) they have been taught to develop a conscious, flexible approach to problem solving and to consult with supervisors and colleagues to gain new perspectives and ideas when current problem-solving efforts seem unproductive.

The social work code of ethics reflects the current professional understanding that competence as a social work practitioner requires a strong base of knowledge and experience. Thus, the second principle of the "conduct and comportment" category, competence and professional development, states that "the social worker should strive to become and remain proficient in professional practice and the performance of professional functions." The code then goes on to specify in further detail that "the social worker should accept responsibility for employment only on the basis of the existing competence or intention to acquire competence," and "the social worker should not misrepresent professional qualifications, education, experience, or affiliation."

At Urban Day, the Director of Social Service brings ideal qualifications to her position. Mrs. Haley earned her master's degree in social work at the branch of the state university located in Project City. As part of her field placement in graduate school, she actually worked at Urban Day as a student social worker. Thus, when hired by Urban Day, Mrs. Haley had completed two years of graduate study in social work which included on-site training specific to the area of developmentally delayed children and the multiple problems of culturally deprived inner-city families. Since graduate school, Mrs. Haley has continued to grow professionally by attending and giving community workshops; by working with a special community project geared toward involving hard-to-reach parents; by developing in-service seminars for Urban Day staff and exchanging information with related agencies; and by serving on boards of directors for other community programs.

Background learning is important for social work, but study must also be ongoing because new practice problems arise on a daily basis. Also, the learning must be assimilated in a form that can be passed on to other staff. For example, Mrs. Haley must coordinate the interactions among children, parents, and staff, and so she must be able to communicate on a variety of levels. Since her own social service staff comprises paraprofessional community workers, she must be able to teach them appropriate skills both verbally and by example. She conducts frequent consultations with these workers regarding specific case situations to teach the purposes and goals of social work intervention and to provide a continual source of support, consultation, and supervision. In addition, Mrs. Haley must be able to communicate with occupational therapists, physical therapists, nurses, speech therapists, psychologists, teachers, psychiatrists, and physicians—at Urban Day as well as related agencies. Communication with volunteers and parents is also important. In short, she has to be able to communicate with everybody involved in a given problem situation and help them communicate with each other.

This process may sound exciting and easy on paper, but one must realize that Mrs. Haley will be the one to persuade the Children's Hospital physician to make another appointment with Ms. Johnston to assess Bobbie and Luann's progress, after Ms. Johnston has missed her appointment for the second time. Mrs. Haley will then have to find a community worker who has the time to go and get Ms. Johnston at home to take her to the appointment, and to make sure she gets there this time. She has to persuade Ms. Johnston to meet with the physician, and perhaps not to drink too much the night before, so that she can have the children ready when the community worker arrives. If Mrs. Haley doesn't do these things herself, she serves as the role model for the staff member who does (for example, Mrs. Dillon). Each communication task involves careful use of language and assessment skills in order to know what needs to be said and who needs to do what to make the desired event occur. Knowledge of community resources is also required, to say nothing of the fact that all this work takes patience and persistence.

Ideally, all of Mrs. Haley's staff would be qualified social workers, too, at least at the accredited BA level. But often, funding levels do not provide sufficient resources. So Mrs. Haley has of necessity hired very carefully selected paraprofessional workers. All the current community workers were originally hired in other positions at Urban Day, two as child-care workers and one as a home trainer. Thus all the social service staff members began their current jobs well informed of the special problems of the clients at Urban Day. They continue their on-the-job training through frequent consultations with Mrs. Haley and with each other, and they also regularly attend the in-service seminars.

In the job of social worker, the interplay of professional and personal characteristics and abilities constantly intermingles. Professional knowledge (for example, about effects of early deprivation on later parenting skills) does help educe patience with a difficult parent from a deprived background. However, sometimes professional knowledge just won't carry the social worker all the way through a trying situation. Understanding the many environmental factors that may influence a response such as unreliable behavior *helps*, but of course it won't eliminate completely the worker's natural response of disappointment and anger. One's personality traits then may become cruical for completing a given task. Perhaps patience and perseverence are the most important characteristics. But why bother to take on such aggravation? Every social worker wonders about this at times! Personal and professional values revolving around the desire for social justice provides some answers. And the reward for patience and persistence also has something to do with the concept of the "small victory"—the proud smile of the mother when she finally makes her own way to the center and observes her child master a new task in physical therapy through the one-way mirror, or the delighted exclamation of the child as he or she succeeds in securing a first oversized button.

PROPRIETY

Let us backtrack slightly now to discuss the first ethical principle concerning conduct and comportment. This principle states: "Propriety—The social worker should maintain high standards of personal conduct in the capacity or identity as social worker." Propriety refers to behavior that would be considered fitting and proper for a social worker on duty. Basically, behavior considered fitting and proper for a social worker on the job would include treating clients with dignity and respect. An example is the self-restraint exhibited by Mrs. Dillon to her client Ms. Johnston on the telephone even when the latter was refusing to get out of bed to put her children on the school bus. Mrs. Dillon could have chosen to abuse Ms. Johnston verbally and then terminate her case. As a social service worker she did not do so and in fact was obligated to search for many other approaches before resorting to termination. Planned confrontation might on occasion be appropriate in the intervention process with Ms. Johnston, but confrontation also should be conducted in a respectful and professional manner.

The code goes on to elaborate that private conduct is a personal matter for the social worker as it is for anyone else. The first provision under the propriety principle states: "The private conduct of the social worker is a personal matter to the same degree as is any other person's except when such conduct compromises the fulfillment of professional responsibilities."

The director of social services at Urban Day, Mrs. Haley, maintains stringent standards for her own private conduct. For example, she used to live in a home she owned in the suburbs but decided to move into a small rented apartment in an integrated neighborhood in the inner city. She has also adopted a child of minority ethnic heritage. These life-style choices are not required by the code of ethics; they are part of Mrs. Haley's private life. They are choices she has freely made in order to make her private and professional lives more consistent. But what if, by contrast, a different social worker at Urban Day should choose, for example, to organize a racist organization in his or her spare time and frequently made racist statements about clients at meetings? This behavior, though part of the private life of the social worker, would compromise professional responsibilities. In this instance, a case could be filed against the worker with the National Association of Social Workers by an aggrieved party.

To help guide social workers in understanding their professional responsibilities in their private time, another provision under the propriety principle states: "The social worker should distinguish clearly between statements and actions made as a private individual and as a representative of the social work profession or an organization or group." Statements made by a social worker outside the context of work may mistakenly be understood to represent an official position of the social worker's employing organization. It is therefore important for a social worker (at work as well as away from work) to make it clear whether an expressed opinion is a personal or an agency position.

Let us return to Mrs. Haley's conduct and comportment as a specific example of one professional's personal choices. In addition to her work at Urban Day, Mrs. Haley does volunteer work. This work involves counseling with a telephone crisis line organized and maintained almost entirely by unpaid personnel. Through her many contacts both at work and in the volunteer setting, Mrs. Haley is able to develop a growing network of friends and professionals who can be tapped as resources in particularly difficult case situations for her clients. She feels that she can make use of her personal experiences in discussions of life options with her clients. Since she herself has taken risks and has lived a variety of life-styles, she can use her experiences in selected self-disclosure in her work. Her point of view is that she must live her ideals, so that clients in tough circumstances will not be able to control her by making her feel guilty about a discrepancy between her ideals and her life-style. She does not want her personal life to be too remote from her clients' own experiences.

For the purposes of this book, it is important to point out again that Mrs. Haley's choices are personal. They are described here to illustrate how one particular social worker carries over professional purposes and values into daily living. Mrs. Haley's choices won't work for everyone. The important thing to remember is that each person must look within to find out what is personally necessary to maintain a viable life-style. Social work practice involves stress and frustration, as well as the sense of accomplishment that helps create a feeling of purpose and worth. After working all day in the city, it may be very important for some social workers to provide themselves with calm emotional input by going home to a peaceful suburban or rural neighborhood, far from the problems that beset them at work.

This is an appropriate place to introduce the important topic of self-care. Self-nurturance and self-care are crucial if the social worker is to continue his or her work over long periods of time. There is a wise saying (origin unknown to this writer) that goes something like this: "If I am not for myself, who will be? If not now, when? And if I am for myself alone, what am I?" In other words, it must be the social worker him- or herself who makes sure that he or she gets the emotional input to keep going. The client cannot provide this input. The client has to cope with too many things already. The worker will be able to derive a certain amount of energy from the small victories, of course, but these will always be too few and too far between to suffice.

The social worker not only *may* choose a way of living in his or her private time that feels rewarding, nurturing, satisfying—he or she *must*. Even Mrs. Haley eventually moved out of her inner city apartment. A series of robberies in the neighborhood, including two in her own apartment, shattered her sense of security and drained some of the energy normally available for work. She reluctantly made the decision that she needed to express her best ideals in another way besides remaining exposed to all the dangers of the inner city. She moved to another apartment, still in the urban environment but in a physically safer location. She now knows personally the circumstances of life with which many of her clients are required to live and has a real understanding of some of the reasons why many of them move so often, as well as why they would be so frustrated with their own more limited options.

What is important for any social worker in terms of working out a private and a professional life-style is a sense of inner harmony about one's personal choices, so that positive energy is available to do one's work well. It is essential that other persons, clients, colleagues, and friends are treated with care and respect, and this takes a lot of energy and time.

SERVICE

The next principle under the conduct and comportment heading of the code of ethics is service. The code reads: "The social worker should regard as primary the service obligation of the social work profession." The code further specifies in various provisions under this principle that the social worker must assume ultimate responsibility for the quality of service she or he provides and must prevent practices that are inhumane or that discriminate against anyone. At Urban Day, Mrs. Haley translates this aspect of the code into the conscious recognition that constantly changing service delivery is necessary to meet the myriad needs of the clients.

It would, for example, be discriminatory and perhaps inhumane to provide services only for those children whose parents are able to transport them to the center themselves. Many of the children who need the services of Urban Day come from families without means of transportation. Only a small percentage of handicapped children could attend the center, probably those least in need; this circumstance would, in effect, discriminate against many of the poorest. For this reason, Urban Day provides door-to-door bus service within a given geographic area. The buses are specially equipped with car seats, each carefully selected to fit the size and physical needs of a particular child. The staff unloads the children one by one at the center and carries them in (or walks with those who can walk).

Under usual circumstances one would expect that door-to-door bus service would make agency services accessible to all eligible children in the area serviced by the busing. But as has already been pointed out by the Johnston case, that isn't so. Some children need additional advocacy by staff, or their parents won't put them on the bus. So when needed, community workers from the social service staff phone parents to remind them about the bus schedule. When parents still fail to act as reminded, staff will provide personal transportation and special meetings to discuss the problem and what might be done to resolve it. In some cases, staff will telephone the parent, or even a neighbor, to awaken the parent daily. In some cases, even that doesn't work. Then special case conferences have to be held to consider the client's entire situation. If the only way the client can get attention is to make sure her child misses the bus in the morning, the staff seeks another way to provide attention to that mother to reinforce positive behavior instead. Is the staff making the mother too dependent by frequent phone calls? Is there a way to help the mother learn to find new sources of attention for herself? The concerns go on and on.

In order to help meet both children's and parents' needs, parents are encouraged to visit Urban Day and watch their children in therapy, in the classroom, or at play. In this way they learn how to teach their children themselves, and they have the opportunity to discuss personal ideas or problems. In some ways, the social service staff has been at odds with some of the other staff regarding their encouraging parents to spend time at the center. Parents of Urban Day children are frequently disheveled and dirty in appearance; some don't smell very good! While this is also true of many of the children, somehow the children, being so small, manage to look cute anyway. The parents don't. Since the agency gives frequent tours to raise private funds, objections have been raised to the social service staff regarding the advisability of urging parents to spend time at Urban Day. The unsightly parents, it is feared, might inhibit the pledging of donations by the more privileged visitors. However, Mrs. Haley and her staff are committed to the concept of participation by parents, regardless of their physical appearance. For one thing, the staff feels that the more the parents understand about their children's needs and the therapy and treatment they receive at the center, the more they can learn to do for the children at home. Also, the social service staff would prefer that parents gain the attention they need themselves through participation at the center, rather than through withdrawal which prompts the staff to pay attention to them under negative circumstances.

The social service staff feels that many parents need so much attention themselves that it is important to provide it at the center. This opinion isn't based on special intuition or some kind of esoteric professional wisdom. According to Mrs. Haley, parents quite openly say at times that they are sick of talking about their children's needs! They want something for themselves! They are having quite a lot of trouble in their own lives, trying to make ends meet, or combating loneliness, or dealing with relationships with significant others. "Sure my kids are important," parents say, some only teenagers themselves, "but what about *me?*"

One problem is that Urban Day Center is really not organized in a way that is conducive to frequent visits from parents. Each classroom teacher has to provide for fifteen or sixteen children, and to coordinate three child-care workers and several volunteers. Interruption of this activity to teach a parent who has dropped in without an appointment how to work with a particular child is difficult, if not impossible. Yet when parents come to the center, the teachers talk with them when they can. It's just not possible to do it consistently.

Another way Urban Day staff tries to meet client needs is by going the second mile, and then the third, with respect to medical and other types of diagnostic appointments. When the children need attention from professionals outside the agency, the staff encourages the families to arrange the appointments. But if the families cannot or will not do so, Urban Day staff gets involved. The ultimate goal is teaching parents how to perform these necessities themselves, but in the interim staff will bend over backwards to make sure the children receive the medical treatment they need. When a parent "graduates" from needing to be taken to appointments to taking care of scheduling them and arranging transportation themselves, Urban Day staff is careful to reinforce this behavior by recognizing it and thanking the parents.

How can it be that a parent of a handicapped child does not acknowledge the need to take that child in for regular medical appointments? In order to understand this, it is necessary to understand the parent. Mrs. Haley explains it this way: If you live in the 1800s dealing only with what you have then, you don't miss what we have in the 1980s. A common exclamation from a parent, for example, in response to urging that she take a child to a medical appointment, is "Nobody ever took *me* to a doctor!" Aside from the many practical difficulties involved in arranging and keeping medical appointments, such as transportation or child care, there is often little understanding of the value of a medical appointment. The average inner-city parent gets nothing obvious in return except a long boring wait in an uncomfortable metal folding chair in a bleak waiting room. Parents may also be confronted with some quick incomprehensible words from an impersonal doctor plus some scribbled phrases on a sheet of paper that usually goes to the agency nurse and into some file somewhere. This appears insignificant to the parent and seems to have no effect on the child. Moreover, the parent who *doesn't* take a child to the doctor receives no negative feedback from either family or friends, as nobody from the peer group expects a parent to go in the first place. That's very different from peer group expectations for parents of children born into the middle class. So Urban Day attempts slowly and gently to teach the value of medical appointments by translating results to the parents in words they can understand. Of course, it doesn't always work. According to Mrs. Haley, parents at Urban Day don't understand the reason for half of the suggestions made by the Urban Day nurse, despite her patient explanations.

Another way Urban Day provides service to clients is through its physical plant. The agency has sought and received private funds to expand its size, so that now there is plenty of space for all the therapies. There are four classrooms, two for infants and two for toddlers, and lots of joint play area within the building. There is also a small but attractive playground outside. The building and the small outdoor playground are so attractive that some staff feel too much money has been and still is being invested in appearance, and that the physical plant was designed to attract private donations of money as much as to accommodate clients. There is certainly some truth to this allegation, but the physical space works. Moreover, volunteers are attracted in numbers, whereas if the place were shabby and dark, probably few people but the staff would be willing to spend time there. Remodeling has involved the installation of lovely windows and skylights, including open play areas inside, so that once within, visitors forget the drab inner city surroundings. They focus instead on light, hanging green plants, and young children, usually a welcome lift to the spirits. For many parents, however, it is certainly possible that the appearance of the center might be alien and thus threatening. Sadly, not many inner-city dwellers are very familiar with light and greenery.

To summarize the response of Urban Day and its social work staff to the service obligation of the profession, the workers consciously maintain as flexible and creative an approach to problem solving as they possibly can. When clients fail to respond to one type of service, the staff will do their best to understand why, and to modify their approach until they can find an effective one. In addition, the physical plant of the agency has been modified to better serve the needs of its handicapped clients.

INTEGRITY

The next topic addressed by the code of ethics is integrity. The code states that "the social worker should act in accordance with the highest standards of professional integrity and impartiality." It adds that the worker should be careful to "resist the influences and pressures that interfere with the exercise of professional discretion and impartial judgement" and "not exploit professional relationships for personal gain."

In some settings, wealthy clients or clients with personal or political clout might possibly tempt a social worker into preferential service in return for some kind of personal gain, such as money or recommendations for position. At Urban Day, however, this potential is almost absent. Most clients are simply too poor to have anything of material value to exchange for preferential treatment.

However, because most clients are very poor and come from culturally deprived backgrounds, it becomes important that the social workers do not exploit the power differential between themselves and their clients. For example, the social status of staff members at Urban Day is considerably greater than that of their clients. Social workers and community workers have paying jobs that classify them as white collar, or middle class. Their clients, on the other hand, are usually unemployed, or on welfare. The social service staff at Urban Day thus must take care not to exploit their higher social status. Even more, within the context of work at Urban Day, social workers hold a position of power with respect to their clients because of the agency structure. If, in addition to the worker–client status differential within the agency, the social worker were to emphasize to the client that he or she also held a higher position in society at large, withdrawal might be the simplest, safest course of action for the client.

In fact, many clients do withdraw from the agency before they ever get involved by simply neglecting to initiate contact when they are referred to Urban Day. Perhaps a large reason why they do this is fear of how they will be treated at the agency or fear of how they will appear to the staff. Many clients recognize that they are not held in very high esteem by society at large, and they tend not to hold themselves in high esteem either. They feel uncomfortable with the idea of becoming visible to a community agency. This is the point at which the social service workers must become involved in active outreach. The social work staff must often work hard to develop close personal relationships with parents. If the children are to be served, the parents need to become willing to get them to Urban Day one way or another!

The close work with parents provided by social service staff at Urban Day often helps the parents overcome their fears of the unknown by making the unknown familiar and desirable. For example, social workers visit the clients' homes, explain who they are and what they do, bring them to the agency personally, show them around, introduce them to other staff, and so on. The personal relationships carefully developed with parents allow the agency to work. What may become a delicate issue, then, is developing and maintaining enough closeness to a parent to help motivate him or her to enroll the handicapped child at the center, without misleading the parent into thinking a new friend has been made for life. This may not sound like a particularly difficult problem, but it certainly can be at Urban Day. Friendship and attention are valued by everyone, but perhaps the deprived client especially needs them. Yet the social work staff cannot offer the parents all the privileges of full friendship. Friends usually have at least the expectation of ready access to each other at any time, especially during personal emergencies. With the dozens of clients and former clients served by each worker at Urban Day, that would involve too many crises and sleepless nights, and would lead to speedy burnout or exhaustion. Maintaining the closeness needed to help clients build trust, without developing expectations that could later be badly disappointed, can involve a delicate balancing act. Clients must be shown that the social work relationship has limits, for example, that the social work role does not involve attending social parties with the client, or being available for evening telephone conversations, loaning money, or providing transportation except for Urban Day affairs. Accomplishing this involves a great deal of skill and personal integrity on the part of the practitioner.

Another relevant issue under the topic of integrity involves use of agency assets such as equipment. Urban Day has an automobile for transporting clients. It should be signed out only for appropriate use. Use of this vehicle could potentially be abused. For that matter, social workers could leave the agency on fabricated home visits and perhaps go shopping instead; this is a risk for any social agency. At Urban Day, the social service staff takes care not to abuse professional privileges. Further, Urban Day's personnel policies facilitate honesty. If, for example, a social service staff worker needs a mental health day, this is considered a valid reason for absence from work equivalent to taking sick leave or a personal day. A staff person isn't forced into the awkward position of making up stories when he or she is unable to handle work on that occasional very bad day everyone experiences.

In maintaining the principle of integrity presented in the code of ethics, then, social workers at Urban Day are careful to avoid exploiting their social status, which is usually higher than that of their clients. They teach clients verbally and by example to understand the limits of the social work relationship. In addition, workers take care to perform their work and to use any necessary equipment appropriately, honestly, and competently.

SCHOLARSHIP AND RESEARCH

The fifth principle of the code under the conduct and comportment heading pertains to scholarship and research. The code states that "the social worker engaged in study and research should be guided by the conventions of scholarly inquiry." This aspect of the code applies directly to the research and writing of this book. To assure confidentiality for agency, staff, and clients, all names and major identifying characteristics have been changed. While the book is about real people and real problems, certain circumstances in each case situation have been altered to maintain the privacy of all involved.

Even so, the Urban Day staff could not but be aware that they were being observed at work in connection with the writing of this book. That raises interesting issues. How do staff feel when their work is being observed by an outsider? At Urban Day, the reaction has been partly pride and partly fear, pride because most of Urban Day's staff is proud of the agency itself, its purpose, and their own work. The fear arises because participation in such a project involves a personal and professional risk—it exposes staff to criticism, for example. If other staff members read the book they may, because they possess inside information, be able to determine whom a particular story or case example is about. This could lead to criticism, and a fear of such criticism could, in turn, discourage participation in the project. After all, Urban Day's staff often deal with the kind of clients other agencies select out in advance, so as to keep the success statistics looking healthy. It is an uncomfortable position to stick your neck out when other people are watching!

There is also the fear, acknowledged by the director of social service at Urban Day, that methods of dealing with handicapped clients from deprived backgrounds may change considerably in the future. If so, Urban Day's program may some day look out of date to scholars and students. This, too, is a potential source of staff reluctance to be used as research subjects.

In general, then, participation in research can make people feel nervous and exposed. However, many professionals also desire to develop personally and professionally through self-examination and wish to consider new ways of doing things, thus contributing to the profession's expanding knowledge base. And this growth-oriented perspective is the one which has prevailed at Urban Day, so that the agency's administration and staff have agreed that its work may be the subject of a book. Moreover, the staff and the agency as a whole have faith that what they do is as good as or better than what is done elsewhere at the present time.

Research and publication are important activities for professionals because they not only result in the expansion of the knowledge base, but the process of research itself generates new thoughts and perspectives within the researchers. The act of writing is stimulating and can help to catalyze new thoughts. The whole experience of research and publication can result in personal as well as professional enrichment if undertaken on topics in which the researchers are truly interested. Conducting research projects in collaboration with others is particularly productive and satisfying.

As a further consideration in research, the code of ethics also states that social workers undertaking this process should carefully consider any possible consequences to the people involved. Participants in research need to take part voluntarily and be protected from any harm. In order to protect the people who are discussed in this book, all names and some major identifying characteristics have been changed, as mentioned before. The agency and all its workers have voluntarily consented to the project.

As part of the author's commitment to supporting the work of Urban Day, even while privately taking issue with some of its practices, certain issues and facts will not be addressed in this book. They will instead continue to be brought to the attention of the appropriate agency staff in a way which protects the agency's ongoing needs as it refines its purposes and goals. In this way, this type of case study can be valuable to the agency as well as to readers of this book.

To summarize, this chapter illustrates how the ethical principles concerning the social worker's conduct and comportment as a social worker are carried out in a real practice setting, Urban Day Center. The major principles involved are propriety, competence and professional development, service, integrity, and scholarship and research. Other settings might manifest these principles in a different way, but this particular set of illustrations can help the reader understand how concrete daily practice reflects more abstract ethical grounding. Chapter 3 will present practice examples illustrating the second major heading of the code, the social worker's ethical responsibility to clients.

REVIEW

The social worker's professional conduct and comportment involves a variety of principles, as discussed in this chapter. To help the student review these principles, the entire first category of principles of the code of ethics, as published by the National Association of Social Workers, is presented below.

THE SOCIAL WORKER'S CONDUCT AND COMPORTMENT AS A SOCIAL WORKER

A. Propriety. The Social Worker should maintain high standards of personal conduct in the capacity or identity as social worker.
1. The private conduct of the social worker is a personal matter to the same degree as is any other person's, except when such conduct compromises the fulfillment of professional responsibilities.
2. The social worker should not participate in, condone, or be associated with dishonesty, fraud, deceit, or misrepresentation.
3. The social worker should distinguish clearly between statements and actions made as a private individual and as a representative of the social work profession or an organization or group.
B. Competence and Professional Development. The social worker should strive to become and remain proficient in professional practice and the performance of professional functions.
1. The social worker should accept responsibility or employment only on the basis of existing competence or the intention to acquire the necessary competence.
2. The social worker should not misrepresent professional qualifications, education, experience, or affiliations.
C. Service. The social worker should regard as primary the service obligation of the social work profession.
1. The social worker should retain ultimate responsibility for the quality and extent of the service that individual assumes, assigns, or performs.
2. The social worker should act to prevent practices that are inhumane or discriminatory against any person or group of persons.
D. Integrity. The social worker should act in accordance with the highest standards of professional integrity and impartiality.
1. The social worker should be alert to and resist the influences and pressures that interfere with the exercise of professional discretion and impartial judgment required for the performance of professional functions.
2. The social worker should not exploit professional relationships for personal gain.
E. Scholarship and Research. The social worker engaged in study and research should be guided by the conventions of scholarly inquiry.
1. The social worker engaged in research should consider carefully its possible consequences for human beings.
2. The social worker engaged in research should ascertain that the consent of participants in the research is voluntary and informed,

without any implied deprivation or penalty for refusal to participate, and with due regard for participants' privacy and dignity.
3. The social worker engaged in research should protect participants from unwarranted physical or mental discomfort, distress, harm, danger, or deprivation.
4. The social worker who engages in the evaluation of services or cases should discuss them only for professional purposes and only with persons directly and professionally concerned with them.
5. Information obtained about participants in research should be treated as confidential.
6. The social worker should take credit only for work actually done in connection with scholarly and research endeavors and credit contributions made by others.

STUDY QUESTIONS

1 How does the case of the Johnston family illustrate the importance of professional education and supervised experience to achieve competence in social work practice?

2 The code of ethics states that "the private conduct of the social worker is a personal matter to the same degree as is any other person's, except when such conduct compromises the fulfillment of professional responsibilities." What types of private conduct do you think might compromise professional social work responsibilities? What kinds of ongoing activities of your own, if any, do you fear might conflict with professional responsibilities? If possible, compare your concerns with those of other students.

3 How do social workers at Urban Day fulfill the service obligation of the social work profession?

4 How does the low socioeconomic status of many of Urban Day's clients relate to the integrity principle of the code?

5 Why might social workers such as those employed at Urban Day be anxious about participating in research? How might they benefit from such research?

The Social Worker's Ethical Responsibility to Clients

Antonia came to Urban Day when she was about a year old. She was a tiny girl of Hispanic descent who can only be described as absolutely darling, with large black eyes and a responsive smile. She had been born with a variety of physical problems: hydrocephaly, clubfeet, and a mild form of spina bifida. Project City Children's Hospital provided her with excellent medical care at birth. Hydrocephalic children suffer from an excess of fluid in the brain. Their heads eventually swell, and pressure from the excess fluid damages the brain. The hospital installed a sophisticated shunt between Antonia's head and a major artery in her neck, which drained out the excess fluid, preventing any injury. Thus she retained normal intelligence, rather than suffering the mental retardation so often associated with hydrocephaly. The intervention for spina bifida was almost as successful, given the grave nature of this anomaly. The spinal column of children born with spina bifida is not completely joined in the lower vertebrae, so nerve impulses cannot travel from one end of the body to the other. Children born with this condition are usually paralyzed from the waist down and lack feeling in the lower part of their bodies. Thanks to sophisticated surgical intervention by Project City Children's Hospital, however, Antonia was not paralyzed from the waist down, although she didn't have any feeling in the lower part of her body.

While it would be difficult, the medical prognosis was that she would eventually be able to walk and to control her bowel and bladder. However, the other congenital deformity, clubfeet, would prevent Antonia from even beginning to learn to walk. Her feet were curled inward so that their soles almost met, and her knees were pushed outward in an awkward position. Children's Hospital referred Antonia and her parents to Urban Day Center while she underwent a series of casting procedures designed to straighten out her feet as much as possible.

While at Urban Day, Antonia's legs and feet were immobilized for a number of months in a series of casts. Urban Day made sure her hygiene needs were met and that her diet was kept balanced to give her the physical stamina to deal with the stress of the casts, and the physical therapy staff worked with her upper body to develop her strength in that region. Throughout the long casting process, Antonia remained cheerful and responsive. When the casts came off, she received extensive physical therapy and careful attention from the teachers and child-care workers, who gradually and gently began to teach her how to walk. She wore special shoes and a leather strap around her waist, with flexible devices called twister cables running between her waist strap and her shoes along both legs, to provide the legs with springlike support. By the time Antonia neared the age of three, she was able to take a few steps with her feet flat on the floor if an adult walked with her and steadied her by holding her hand. She walked with her feet wide apart, swaying from side to side, but sometimes she even took a step or two on her own. Antonia's shy smile as she toddled hesitantly down the hallway at Urban Day became a familiar and joyful sight.

PRIMACY OF CLIENTS' INTERESTS

If it weren't for the client and the client's needs, the social worker wouldn't be in practice. It is to assist in problem solving with and for the client that the social worker is employed. Therefore, client interests must come first. This obligation is the focus of the second section of the code of ethics, the social worker's ethical responsibility to clients. Under this heading the code includes four principles. The first, primacy of clients' interests, states that "the social worker's primary responsibility is to clients." This principle of the code includes eleven provisions, the first of which instructs: "The social worker should serve clients with devotion, loyalty, determination, and the maximum application of professional skill and competence." Let us return to the case of little Antonia to illustrate how this principle and its provisions apply in a real practice situation.

Antonia eventually approached the age of three, at which she could not remain at Urban Day because the agency is not eligible for funding for children over three. Further service would have to be provided through the special education programs of the public schools. When any child at Urban Day turns two years and nine months of age and still has special needs, it is the agency's policy to contact the public schools. This contact is made by the social service staff, and the timing allows the schools three months to conduct their own evaluation, the maximum allowed by law to evaluate a special education referral. In this way, there need not be a break in service between the time the child leaves Urban Day and enters the public school programs.

Since Antonia clearly was in need of further physical therapy and assistance in learning to walk, Emily Gantz, the Urban Day community worker assigned to her case, contacted the public schools when Antonia was two years and nine months of age. The little girl was accepted by the special education program for service. Emily was assured that Antonia would be enrolled in an early intervention program and receive regular physical therapy.

Even before Emily contacted the public schools, she made an appointment to talk with Antonia's mother, Mrs. Salazar, about the fact that her daughter soon would be too old to be eligible for Urban Day's services. She explained to Mrs. Salazar that Antonia would probably be eligible for services by the public schools if the mother would consent to such service. This personal contact by Emily is in accord with provisions six and nine under the primacy of clients' interests principle of the code of ethics, which state, respectively: "The social worker should provide clients with accurate and complete information regarding the extent and nature of the services available to them," and "the social worker who anticipates the termination or interruption of service to clients should notify clients promptly and seek the transfer, referral, or continuation of service in relation to the client's needs and preference." In fact, Emily had informed Antonia's family of Urban Day's age limit from the very beginning of her contacts with them, and had reminded them throughout Antonia's treatment. Antonia's mother, fully informed as to the reasons, consented to her daughter's enrollment in the public school special education program. She signed the required forms and sent them on to the public schools.

It is relevant to point out here that while Antonia was the client needing treatment in this case, it was her parents who had the legal right to make decisions regarding what was done for her, since she was a legal minor. Hence the careful work with the parents by Urban Day. Under the second principle, rights and prerogatives of clients, of the second section of the code of ethics, provision number two states: "When another individual has been legally authorized to act in behalf of a client, the social worker should deal with that person always with the client's best interests in mind." By dealing frequently and respectfully with Antonia's parents, Mrs. Gantz was keeping the little girl's best interests in mind as required by the code.

Shortly after Antonia left Urban Day, Emily called the public schools to make sure the treatment plans were operating smoothly. She learned that the little girl was attending special classes, but was unable to determine if Antonia was also receiving physical therapy. After calling several times without obtaining a definite answer, Emily began to have the vague, uneasy feeling she was being put off. Finally, she had one of Urban Day's physical therapists call the physical therapist at the school. Urban Day's physical therapist got through and was assured that treatment had indeed begun.

Emily relaxed with the soothing knowledge that one little child had gained the ability to walk at Urban Day and that her progress would be maintained in the public preschool program. Perhaps by the time Antonia was old enough for kindergarten, she would be close enough to normal to enroll in a regular classroom. Emily completed the paperwork to formally close Antonia's case at Urban Day. Success stories like this are treasured because, of course, things don't always work out so nicely.

A couple of months passed, and then the bubble of success broke. In talking with a social worker at the public schools about another case, Emily asked casually if the worker knew how Antonia's therapy was progressing. The school worker said equally casually that he wasn't sure therapy had started; he hadn't seen any orders for that service. At about the same time, a social worker at Children's Hospital called Emily to talk about Antonia, as she had just been assigned the little girl's case due to a hospital reorganization and wanted to bring the transferred records up to date. Emily supplied the needed discharge information from Urban Day and then asked the worker in return if she would check the Children's Hospital records to see if an order for physical therapy for Antonia had been sent to the public schools. It had. Armed with this information, Emily called the public schools again and this time reached the physical therapist. In answer to her direct question whether Antonia was receiving physical therapy, the therapist's answer was simply "no." When Emily asked why, the response was that the two letters of authorization were missing—one from Children's Hospital and one from the mother. Emily was horrified. "Did you contact the mother or the hospital to try to obtain that authorization?" she asked. "No," the therapist said shortly. "Why?" came the logical ensuing query. The therapist's answer was somewhat defensive, but included the opinion that a responsible mother would provide the necessary signed forms to authorize therapy without having to be actively pursued.

To make a long story short, from Emily's best reconstruction of events, both the hospital and the mother sent the required signed forms to the schools, but the schools either did not receive them or else misplaced them. In any event, Antonia did not receive treatment. Part of the reason may have been one professional's opinion that parents who are thought to be unreliable deserve not to have their children served, or else that children of parents thought to be unreliable do not deserve to be served. In fact, his feelings may have been so strongly slanted against families he perceived to be undeserving that he deliberately misled the Urban Day staff when they called to make sure Antonia was receiving physical therapy.

Antonia's Hispanic parents did not feel self-assured around Anglo institutions like public schools. Their English was limited. They needed active outreach as provided by Urban Day to encourage them to visit their daughter at school to learn firsthand what services she was receiving there. No such active outreach was provided by the staff at the public schools. So there was no one else to investigate for little Antonia when the physical therapist misinformed the Urban Day staff.

Refusing to Condone Discrimination

Relevant to this story is the third provision under the primacy of clients' interests principle of the code: "The social worker should not practice, condone, facilitate, or collaborate with any form of discrimination on the basis of race, color, sex, sexual orientation, age, religion, national origin, marital status, political belief, mental or physical handicap, or any other preference or personal characteristics, condition, or status."

Antonia was very probably discriminated against, via disastrous neglect, on the basis of her race, color, national origin, and the personal characteristic, condition, or status known as lower social class or poverty. Once Mrs. Gantz realized what was happening, she refused to condone or collaborate with this neglect and began active advocacy for the little girl. Emily's active intervention and pursuit of the case through the special education supervisors at the public schools got Antonia's therapy started again.

But Antonia's regression was severe. While going to her special program every day but without anyone in the new program advocating in her behalf to get the physical therapy started, she lost a great deal of ground. One foot is totally clubbed again, and she can no longer walk. In a mere two and a half months of interruption in service, Antonia lost the benefit of about two years of work and will have to go back into her casts again. And since she is over three years of age now, her bones will not be as flexible as they were when she was an infant; the correction probably cannot be as complete as it once was. But at least the treatment has started again, due to the persistent efforts of an Urban Day social service staff member *after* the case had been transferred to another agency at which time all formal responsibility for Antonia's treatment program had ceased. This is certainly an example of social service where the primacy of clients' interests was recognized and practiced. Emily Gantz is still involved as this chapter is being written, advocating to have Antonia transferred to a different special education program where she can receive physical therapy from a professional with a different emotional orientation towards her and her family. She is also involved in arranging a legal medical guardian for the little girl, to ensure continued active advocacy for Antonia when Urban Day's involvement ceases.

Serving with Determination

The first provision under the primacy of clients' interests principle of the code, as noted previously, states: "The social worker should serve clients with devotion, loyalty, determination, and the maximum application of professional skill and competence." A particular example of serving clients with loyalty and determination may be advocacy, as illustrated in the example of little Antonia. Urban Day staff begins advocating on behalf of potential clients' interests upon initial contact. One way the staff does so is by keeping up to date with respect to the criteria used by the county Combined Community Services Board (CCSB) for accepting cases for funding. At one time in the very recent past, Urban Day was considered by the Board as *the* place to send all handicapped children, as long as there was likely to be an opening in the not too distant future. Now, however, as mentioned earlier, saving dollars in the short run is the name of the funding game. All children evaluated by the Central Referral Committee are sent to the half-day agencies in the interest of saving money, unless there is some obvious overriding reason why a particular child must receive services for a full day, because the CCSB will not fund more than half a day's treatment except under special circumstances.

Lately, according to Mrs. Haley, the criteria considered acceptable by the CCSB for funding a child for service at Urban Day relate not to the extent of the child's handicap but to the child's family circumstances. If the family situation involves clear and present danger to the child, then he or she is likely to be approved for service at Urban Day. If the child has overwhelming physical or intellectual needs, but his or her family is relatively intact, then that child is likely to be sent to a half-day program. Mrs. Haley has requested a number of times that the changing funding criteria be explained in more detail, but the answer she receives from the Chairperson of the Combined Community Services Board is, to quote verbatim, "It's just not that black and white."

In the mid-1970s, when public funding for treatment of children with developmental disabilities was relatively plentiful, extensively handicapped children were approved for funding at Urban Day without question. In preparing documentation to verify the need for service, Urban Day social service staff became accustomed to focusing on the children's developmental needs. If there were overwhelming risks of abuse or neglect in the family situation, these were documented as well, but the philosophy of the Urban Day staff was and still is to search out and reinforce the strengths, not the weaknesses, in each family. Staff looked for strengths from the initial meetings with the families, even the most troubled. This orientation maximizes potential for positive change and helps workers serve clients with maximum "devotion, loyalty, and determination." So the agency's documentation stressed the children's developmental needs but also emphasized family strengths. Over time, the social service staff learned what kind of developmental needs were consistently approved for funding, so that they could begin to work with appropriate families with reasonable assurance that work together would continue on a regular basis. That helped establish a bond of commitment between staff and client from the very beginning of service.

In the early 1980s, however, several children with extensive developmental delays were suddenly denied funding at Urban Day. These children met all the usual criteria for acceptance and the director of social services, Mrs. Haley, was shocked. She was also placed in an awkward position because, her previous experience having taught her that children like these would be approved, she had already developed a trusting relationship with the children's parents. One child was even receiving treatment, pending the expected routine authorization for funding. But suddenly, the funding doors were slammed shut. The explanation of the funding body, the Combined Community Services Board, as to why these children were rejected was fuzzy. "It's just not that black and white," was all Mrs. Haley was told. Needless to say, such a response in such a difficult circumstance was not particularly satisfactory. In due course, new funding criteria became clearer as the Central Referral Committee, to which Urban Day then sent a representative, began to send more and more children to the half-day agencies, unless the children came from families with documented abuse.

Mrs. Haley went to the head of the Combined Community Services Board to discuss the situation. She pointed out the need for clear funding criteria to avoid misleading potential new referrals, and she attempted to contest the apparent necessity for children to come from abusing families in order to be accepted for funding. The Chairperson of the Board was willing to listen, but shared with Mrs. Haley her own constraints. "You have to understand that I'm in a bind," she said. "With all the funding cuts from the federal and state governments, I have to justify to the county why we are approving each child for any given program. There has to be a strong reason why we approve a child for a full day of treatment when half a day might do. You really don't *want* us to specify exact criteria, because that would cut out all flexibility."

Under the circumstances, according to Mrs. Haley, perhaps it *is* a good idea that funding criteria aren't totally defined by the county at this time, because that might cut out the possibility of advocating for an exception you believe in. For example, under the apparent but unwritten current guidelines for funding, Don Green, the little child with Down's syndrome discussed in the first chapter, shouldn't have been approved. Don's parents have an intact marriage, there is no child abuse, and both parents work at full-time professional jobs, so the family has a good income. However, as Mrs. Haley pointed out, full-day child care was a pressing need for the family when they applied. There wasn't a day-care center in the county that would have accepted Don. He had heart problems, needed special medication all day long, and had feeding problems. Besides low motivation for feeding, most of the food that made its way down to his stomach came back up. Due to low muscle tone, he needed a lot of individual stimulation to move his hands, turn over, smile. He couldn't give caretakers much reward for their efforts. For a professionally active mother or father to have to give up a career to spend twenty-four hours a day at home caring for such a handicapped child could be emotionally crippling. While it could be argued that the Greens had an ideal family situation to take care of their own needs, in reality, they were as in need of help as an abusive family, only in their own particular way. Placement could help the family cope and actively prevent deterioration. As it happened, little Don died of his heart problems after a few months. Mrs. Haley remained actively involved in counseling with the parents for a period of time thereafter, helping them deal with the death. Sometimes a death that is partially desired is as hard to cope with as any other or more so, due to feelings of guilt as well as sadness.

The placement of little Don Green at Urban Day was a direct result of the active advocacy of the social service staff, who kept as abreast of the funding criteria as possible and learned to word application forms in as sophisticated and timely a manner as possible. In Don's case, the argument was made that the complexity of his medical needs were such that no other facility in the county could meet them for a full day.

Another child admitted for service to the center due to the active advocacy of the staff was Hunter Walsh. Hunter's parents referred the boy themselves. He had a seizure disorder and had been receiving services at one of the half-day agencies in Project City. Dissatisfied with his treatment there, the parents had removed the little boy from that program. The staff wouldn't explain to the parents what types of therapy the little boy was receiving and why; and at one point a staff member called the mother a klutz. Understandably, that hurt her feelings. As she explained to Mrs. Haley, "I guess I am a klutz sometimes, but I like to be treated with respect."

The Walsh parents toured Urban Day and became excited about the program there. They wanted to enroll little Hunter. Hunter's seizures were serious enough that Mrs. Haley knew he would have been approved for funding only a short time ago, but now she doubted it—not because Hunter didn't need special services, but because the parents were still together and did not abuse the child. So she did what she knew she had to do in order to obtain funding for the family. She searched for weaknesses. She found out everything she could that would make the family look bad. And then she wrote up the application stressing the problems, including the fact that they had been involved with protective services at one time in another state. That did it. Hunter was now portrayed not just as a child with special physical needs but as a child at risk. And he received funding.

Mrs. Haley has explained candidly to the head of the Combined Community Services Board how much she dislikes being put in the position of having to search for family weaknesses. Ethically the practice creates a dilemma, because she must slant reality if she hopes to obtain funding.

And somehow, even though technically the practice of looking for weaknesses may only be learning to play the funding game, the actual experience of doing this changes one's mind-set toward the family. Now, somehow, the family looks worse than it did at first. The weaknesses are written down and highlighted in black and white. Mrs. Haley says that her social service staff has such a long history of looking for family strengths that once a family is approved for funding, the members can generally manage to shift gears out of the pathology model (or the treatment model which stresses what is wrong or sick, rather than what is right or healthy). But she is afraid that students will not be able to make this transition, and she feels this is a real problem. There are enough people in this society who perceive the fault to lie in the inherent capacities of the victim without training students to look for what is bad in their clients. But is it more ethical to deny a family service by not playing the funding game when they meet the criteria for service as established by the agency itself?

The Greens and the Walshes present real-life ethical dilemmas in which responsible social workers might argue for very different approaches to service. One approach could be to present the prospective clients to the Combined Community Services Board in a manner that emphasizes their strengths. This approach would be considered professionally preferable because it maximizes the potential for constructive work with the clients. However, as pointed out above, under current social and economic circumstances this approach would effectively disqualify many clients for funding at Urban Day. The other approach would be to present prospective clients to the Combined Community Service Board in a way that emphasized negative factors, especially parental abuse. This approach would not ordinarily be professionally recommended because it creates negative expectations for the family which can become self-fulfilling prophesies. However, this approach provides the greatest chance for funding at present.

At Urban Day, this ethical dilemma remains active in everyone's mind, but in practice it has been resolved by opting for the second approach. Practically speaking, it does little good to create the best possible atmosphere for work with prospective clients if they don't get funded for service. So the social service staff makes its case on behalf of prospective clients in the way it believes most likely to result in funding. Thereafter, the agency must consciously debrief itself to overcome the negative effects of this tactic.

Uncertain funding criteria also delay development of meaningful relationships with parents. If staff have to be very tentative in their initial contacts with a family, the bonding so helpful in enabling parents to participate in Urban Day's program is delayed. And as the more astute parents ask how likely it is that their child will be funded, the staff cannot say, "We're sorry, but we don't think you are quite abusive enough," or "Oh boy, we may be able to make you look abusing enough to make it."

Instead, they respond by saying, "We can't really tell you," a response which may seem to be a put-off to the parents. And the staff tend to keep their distance, too, because they do not want to seem to be making a commitment to a family when funding may so easily be denied. A few unforeseen funding refusals have made all initial contacts tentative, for protection of both worker and client.

In an effort to avoid focusing on negatives and serving children only from abusing families, the social service staff has been discussing the possibility of changing agency policy to accept children whose parents would pay all or part of their tuition. So far this is not possible due to restrictions from earlier funding sources, but the agency as a whole is giving consideration to this option in the future. The danger, of course, would be that if all families were required to pay *some* part of the fee, those clients living below the poverty line would be powerfully deterred from enrollment, and that is the majority of Urban Day's clientele at this time. Urban Day charged its parents two dollars per day at one time for its bus service, obviously far below agency cost. But even this charge deterred many parents from sending their children. To a middle-class person it seems absurd that a two dollars per day charge could deter a family's participation, but that translates into a monthly charge of over forty dollars. By comparison, the family budget from Aid to Families with Dependent Children is increased by only about seventy dollars per month when a new baby is born, at least in the state where Urban Day is located.

Apprising Clients of Risks, Rights, and Opportunities

So far this chapter has talked about situations where Urban Day advocated to the best of its ability to obtain funding so that it could serve its clients for a full day. However, at times Urban Day staff has questioned the advisability of keeping a child in its program for a full day. In fact, on rare occasions Urban Day social service staff has advocated on behalf of potential clients so that they will *not* have to enroll at Urban Day, or at least that their enrollment will be time-limited. How can this be?

As an example, let us examine the case of the Evans family. Cora Evans was a fifteen-year-old black woman who became pregnant by her boyfriend when she was in the tenth grade. Both of the teenage parents were average students and planned to complete high school. But when Cora gave birth to not one baby but two, and both were born with problems, she decided to become a full-time mother. Fortunately, Cora's own mother permitted her to live at home, even though the house was already crowded, being shared by several members of the extended family. Ten people in all, including an aunt, uncle, and Cora's grandmother, lived in the family home, a two-story, four-bedroom frame house owned by the grandmother. Pooling resources is an important way people survive in the inner city.

Cora and her boyfriend Willy had a supportive relationship, but the young couple did not feel ready to marry. Being slightly overweight and naive, Cora did not even know she was pregnant until she was almost five months along, when her friends began to tease her. Willy could not provide monetary support, so Cora applied for and received a grant from Aid to Families with Dependent Children. Cora was excited and happy when the twins were born. However, as is very common with teenage pregnancies, they were premature. Willy Jr. weighed only three and one-half pounds and Charlie three pounds, nine ounces. Both had to be taken to the intensive care unit right after birth.

Cora went through a frightening week in which her two new sons developed hyperbilirubinemia, a malfunction of the liver leading to jaundice, for which they were treated with photo (light) therapy. They also required special intravenous feedings because they could not suck strongly enough to get milk out of a nipple, and they had to be kept in an incubator because they needed oxygen. Within a week the bilirubin count was normal, but the children remained in the hospital for six weeks before gaining enough weight to be permitted go to home. The whole experience was bewildering and frightening for Cora who had never heard of such terrifying terms as hyperbilirubinemia and found it hard to understand the medical explanations. It was also frightening to see such tiny human beings kept inside an incubator attached to all sorts of tubes. Cora was glad to get her sons home and hoped that she would never need to take the children to a hospital again.

But the twins kept spitting up their milk. The spitting up became excessive one night and Cora's mother suggested the girl take them to the hospital for a checkup. Cora took them to the closest hospital emergency room. She had a long wait there, and when a doctor finally examined her children, he told her nothing was wrong. He told her to see her regular doctor about a formula change if the spitting up continued. Cora was relieved and went home. However, two days later the children continued to spit up most of their food and seemed quite weak, so she called and made an appointment at the infants' regular clinic at Children's Hospital.

When she arrived for her appointment two days later, both children appeared very sickly. The doctor in the infant's clinic took one look at them and began to reprimand her for keeping them at home so long. He asked her rudely if she was feeding them at all, and then, without listening to her answer, began to berate her. Among other things, he told Cora she was an unfit mother. Then he informed her he was admitting both children to the hospital immediately, and that she must call her own mother to come down and sign the required papers, as she was underage.

Cora was ashamed, frightened, and angry. Of course she had been feeding her babies, or at least trying to. Only recently she had been assured by another doctor that her children were all right. But she called her own mother and had the children admitted to the hospital; she stayed with them most of the time, watching Willy Jr. and Charlie receiving sustenance by tube again, not a happy sight. In the morning, Cora received a visit from the hospital social worker. The hospital social worker told her in a straightforward way that she was being referred to Blue County Protective Services as a case of apparent child neglect. At this point Cora, exhausted and upset from lack of sleep in strange surroundings, became very angry. By the time the protective services worker arrived, she was hostile and defensive, blaming the doctor, the nurse, the social worker, anyone in the world but herself for the condition of her children. Her angry, acccusing langauge only undermined her credibility, and her disheveled appearance supported a case for neglect. The protective services worker sought and received a temporary court order to have the twins removed from the mother's custody to a foster home.

Cora's reaction was to protest quite directly. She took her children home from the hospital without a discharge order and when the police came to get them, she put one twin under each arm and took off down the street as fast as a spirited, healthy teenager could run. But it wasn't quite fast enough. She was caught, and the children were taken away and put into foster care under highly charged circumstances. Cora's behavior, of course, didn't improve protective service's evaluation of her performance as a mother!

Willy Jr. and Charlie were then referred to Urban Day by the protective services worker, who highly respected the agency's abilities to work with problem parents as well as children. Cora was sincerely described in the referral report as an uncaring, unloving parent, an adolescent who didn't even bother to feed her own children. The reasons cited for referral included child neglect, inadequate nutrition, developmental delays, and lack of bonding between mother and children.

Mrs. Haley took care to examine with special attention all cases referred to Urban Day for inadequate bonding issues. Bonding is a term used to describe the close emotional relationship between parent and child that is probably required to motivate the parent to meet a child's ongoing needs. In Mrs. Haley's opinion, taking children out of the home for a full day as a means for treating bonding problems could be exactly the wrong thing to do. Sometimes, to be sure, day treatment could allow a parent to invest quality time in the children in the mornings and evenings rather than being overwhelmed all day long. But equally likely, bonding could be inhibited by so many hours of absence from the home. So when Mrs. Haley had her first interview with Cora, she listened to this mother and her story very carefully.

By this time Cora, while still upset and angry, had calmed down considerably. She was beginning, in a way, to feel defeated rather than rebellious. She told her story to Mrs. Haley in a coherent fashion, and

Mrs. Haley decided to believe her. Mrs. Haley consciously decides to believe her clients under most circumstances. "Sure," she says, "I can be snowed and I know it. But I start with the assumption of truth and work from there because I think trust is mutual. If I trust the clients they are more likely to trust me, and then we can work better with each other."

"Failure to thrive" is a term used to describe children who may, through no fault of the parents, appear severely neglected and malnourished. In fact, they *are* malnourished. But they may be eating regularly, throwing all the food up for some reason. In this case, what Cora told Mrs. Haley led Mrs. Haley to believe that "failure to thrive" might be the correct diagnosis for these children. Cora told Mrs. Haley of the nights she had stayed up all the way through until morning feeding the twins, trying to get the food to stay down. Mrs. Haley believed her. Now she needed to decide how best to handle this referral.

There are several provisions under the code of ethics primacy of clients' interests principle that could be applied to a case like Cora Evans's. Numbers six and seven are particularly pertinent. Number six, as noted previously, states that "the social worker should provide clients with accurate and complete information regarding the extent and nature of services available to them," and number seven states that "the social worker should apprise clients of their risks, rights, opportunities, and obligations associated with social service to them."

Since Cora Evans came to Urban Day as an involuntary client, under court order through Blue County Protective Services, she would not know when she arrived that Urban Day could truly help her. She was simply afraid of losing her children—in fact, she had. They were already in foster care, and Urban Day seemed to be part of that process. She arrived at the agency highly anxious. Mrs. Haley's first task was to let Cora tell her story and to assure her that it was heard and respected. Accepting Cora's story would help the girl become less defensive. Then Mrs. Haley's task was to describe for the young mother the services Urban Day had to offer both her and the twins, as well as to clarify the current role of protective services in her case. Mrs. Haley explained to Cora that while she personally believed the girl's story regarding her responsible care for Willy Jr. and Charlie, that at this point in time protective services did not, and that they had enough circumstantial evidence to the contrary (the malnourished condition of the twins, as well as Cora's abducting them from the hospital) to convince the court that Cora was an unfit mother.

During this process Mrs. Haley consulted with the protective services worker, expressing the professional opinion that Cora was not an unfit mother, and that in fact full-day placement at Urban Day might not be an appropriate plan for the twins, as it could interfere with maternal bonding. But the worker insisted on placement at least for enough time to undertake more in-depth assessment. That plan seemed reasonable to Mrs. Haley, who then explained the worker's position to Cora. Protective services was willing to allow Urban Day to provide Cora with social service supervision rather than providing it themselves if Cora would participate actively in Urban Day's program. Protective services would terminate their involvement entirely if Mrs. Haley recommended that they do so after a reasonable period of time. Mrs. Haley told Cora in a sympathetic way that the girl's primary task now should be to demonstrate that she *could* be a responsible mother, and that Urban Day would help her to do so if she wished.

Cora Evans felt that she would much prefer to have her children at home and attending Urban Day than to leave them in a foster home. In this way she changed her position from that of potential involuntary client to a voluntary one. What she would have preferred, of course, would be to have them at home with her all day. Mrs. Haley personally felt that Cora's wishes made sense and would have liked to honor them. The best plan of all in Mrs. Haley's estimation would have been to return the children to Cora Evans but have them come to Urban Day for half-day treatment. However, this option was not available. Protective services was not willing to return the children to the home without supervised programming at Urban Day, and Urban Day did not have a half-day option.

Mrs. Haley had Charlie and Willy Jr. evaluated by the Urban Day staff. Their intellectual functioning appeared normal but there were delays in physical development that did warrant treatment, related to the premature birth and current malnutrition. Urban Day decided to accept the children for service and then advocate with protective services to have the children returned to their natural mother, which occurred shortly thereafter.

The case of Cora Evans and her twins worked out well. To help facilitate bonding, the Urban Day staff encouraged Cora to come to the center regularly to work with the children. She was happy and willing to do so. The Urban Day nurse worked carefully with Cora to devise a feeding schedule that involved frequent small portions. In time, the children began to gain weight. With physical therapy and stimulation in the classroom, they were soon healthy and active. With encouragement by the Urban Day staff, Cora herself began to think about returning to school and eventually decided to take courses to prepare herself to become a beautician. Long before the children left Urban Day, they were released from protective services supervision. When their weight and behavior were within the normal range, they continued briefly at Urban Day to stabilize their gains and then enrolled part-time in a regular day-care center. The mother was involved in all the related planning, so that when the children were terminated at Urban Day, the next steps in their plan of care had been worked out carefully in advance. Thus Cora Evans, carefully informed by Mrs. Haley of the risks, rights, opportunities, and obligations associated with participating in the program at Urban Day, voluntarily decided to take part. The results were demonstrably positive.

Termination

In the code of ethics under the principle, primacy of clients' interests, three provisions deal with termination. Provision nine reads: "The social worker should terminate service to clients, and professional relationships with them, when such service and relationships are no longer required or no longer serve the clients' needs or interests." Provision ten states: "The social worker should withdraw services precipitously only under unusual circumstances, giving careful consideration to all factors in the situation and taking care to minimize possible adverse affects." Provision eleven further specifies (as noted previously in the Antonia Salazar case): "The social worker who anticipates the termination or interruption of service to clients should notify clients promptly and seek the transfer, referral, or continuation of service in relation to the clients' needs and preferences."

At Urban Day, the issue of when to terminate is sometimes a tough one. Sometimes children are brought up to normal age level in terms of their physical and mental development, but they are not yet three years of age. There is no program to send them where they can maintain the gains in functioning, however. In these cases the children are sometimes terminated and sometimes not, the decision being made on a case-by-case basis according to Urban Day's best professional estimate of whether the children's families are capable of maintaining the gains. In no case is a child precipitously terminated without careful planning along with the parent or parents involved. Whenever possible and appropriate, resources from outside Urban Day are brought in to continue some service after discharge. For example, a public health nurse may continue to work with the family on hygiene issues. But sometimes the issue of termination is difficult for another reason besides the professional goal of maintaining the child's physical and intellectual skills. Sometimes the family simply neglects to bring the child in for service, and at a certain point the case must be terminated so that the energy invested in struggling with that family can be reinvested in more productive situations. This is an extremely difficult decision for Urban Day staff. Termination under these circumstances is a measure of last resort.

Such a case was that of Michelle Champlin. Michelle was referred to Urban Day by Blue County Protective Services because of reported child abuse and neglect. The family situation was not abusive enough, in the estimation of the protective services worker, to warrant removing the child from the home. Strong, visible evidence of abuse such as bruises or lacerations are usually required for removal, or evidence of virtual starvation, as in the case of the Evans twins. However, the worker felt that Michelle was delayed and that the delay was due to lack of stimulation. The home represented a high-risk environment due to the rejecting attitude of the mother combined with the large number of children.

Urban Day tested Michelle and found her speech and physical

development were indeed delayed. The delay did not seem due to any genetic handicap but rather to lack of attention and stimulation at home. As the Urban Day staff began to work with Michelle, they visited the mother frequently. She had several other young children in the home and Michelle was the only one obviously delayed. The mother made it clear that she did not like this particular daughter, screaming at her frequently when anything went wrong and ignoring her the rest of the time. The abuse noted was not physical but psychological. Michelle was withdrawn and almost totally nonverbal in response. At Urban Day, however, the little girl began to interact socially bit by bit as she gained confidence.

At first Mrs. Haley felt positive about the likelihood that Mrs. Champlin, a middle-aged woman with a bitter attitude toward life, perhaps because of her husband's desertion of her, would send Michelle to Urban Day regularly. After all, that would get the little girl away from home, and Mrs. Champlin did not like the child. But perhaps unfortunately, Michelle made no trouble at home. She rarely made any noise, and played off by herself in a corner. Sometimes she just sat alone in the corner without doing anything at all. She took virtually no mothering time, and yet she was there to be yelled at when the mother was frustrated.

For a short time, Michelle came to Urban Day fairly regularly, and with the careful attention of the speech therapists her language patterns began to improve. She interacted regularly with staff and other children. She improved dramatically with positive attention, rewarding the staff with measurable gains for relatively little work. But then she stopped coming.

Mrs. Dillon had a number of conferences with the mother to learn the reason and was told that Mrs. Champlin couldn't wake up early enough in the morning to get Michelle on the bus. So Mrs. Dillon, a diligent worker, called the mother on the telephone every morning to alert her to the imminent arrival of the bus. Soon the Champlin telephone was disconnected! Mrs. Dillon made more personal visits to the Champlin home and received assurances that the child would be sent the very next day. But she wouldn't be on the bus the next day. Mrs. Dillon would go out to transport Michelle in person and would find herself coping with an extremely unpleasant mother at the home scene. It became clear that Mrs. Champlin actively resented the intervention of Urban Day. She wanted to be left alone. She wanted social workers out of her life. She knew what she was doing. Her child didn't need special services, in her opinion. She finally said so very clearly.

Mrs. Dillon tried to bring Blue County Protective Services back into the case. They refused because they said Urban Day's own tests showed the child to be almost up to age level by now. This was true. But the Urban Day staff expected that in her hostile home environment, nonverbal and social withdrawal behavior would again be required of Michelle on a regular basis, and she would lose the progress she had gained. That, however, wasn't an adequate argument to warrant a new protective services order.

Protective services programs in most states, including the one in which Urban Day is located, are crisis oriented. In general, the laws governing protective service require substantial evidence of abuse to children before the courts can step in. In all but the worst cases, protective services is unable to intervene even when the workers *want* to protect a child known to be at risk. Laws protecting children are weak, in general, probably because the parents who make the laws are ambivalent about passing any legislation that might be used to limit what they perceive as their parental rights. In addition, the programs that do exist are often weakly funded, resulting in the hiring of inadequate numbers of workers. Those who hold the existing positions are burdened by impossibly large caseloads, requiring workers to focus only on the worst situations. Inadequate legislation and inadequate funding to protect children is of course an ethical issue at the societal level. Its effects on individuals are illustrated time and time again by the little persons who become the primary clients at Urban Day, or who do *not* become the clients even though a need exists.

Maintenance of normal behavior and prevention of abuse in noncrisis situations, then, is not the public mandate of county protective services. Urban Day, by contrast, is philosophically vested in prevention of deterioration as well as in remedying delay. And since Michelle was not quite up to age level in some of her verbal and physical skills, the center could still obtain funding for her treatment. So the staff invested an enormous amount of energy in encouraging Mrs. Champlin to send Michelle to the center. The staff knew that without Urban Day's active intervention, Mrs. Champlin would be Michelle's entire world, and that world was alternately ignoring, rejecting, and otherwise psychologically abusive. The social service staff hated to abandon the child to that kind of environment.

However, the day came when Mrs. Dillon recognized she was channeling a great deal of energy and time into a case situation where she was making absolutely no headway. It felt to her as if she had been hitting her head against a wall for a long time, and the wall hadn't moved one inch. In fact, it was growing thicker by the day. Mrs. Champlin was beginning to refuse to answer the door as well as the telephone by now. Were the returns worth the time and energy? Michelle was only one child in Mrs. Dillon's caseload; some other cases were quite promising but needed more time and attention to assure best results.

In this case situation Mrs. Dillon felt like a truant officer, unwanted and ineffective. In other cases, she was welcome and able to provide more service with less investment. She wasn't sure what she should do. So she consulted with Mrs. Haley. By so doing she was observing the eighth provision under the primacy of clients' interests principle of the code of ethics: "The social worker should seek advice and counsel of colleagues and supervisors whenever such consultation is in the best interests of clients."

Mrs. Dillon and Mrs. Haley discussed the Champlin case for a few weeks before finally deciding that termination was the appropriate course of action. The only way the agency could enforce attendance with any client was to threaten termination as the last resort. And in this case, it was known in advance that this was precisely what this mother *wanted*. The agency had no way to make Mrs. Champlin send little Michelle. The staff was powerless unless Blue County Protective Services was willing to intervene. The staff agonized about the case because they did not think termination would be a good plan for Michelle. They tried to find other appropriate resources that Mrs. Champlin would work with, such as a family counseling agency, but they couldn't come up with any.

As required by the code of ethics, in particular the seventh provision under the primacy of clients' interests principle, Mrs. Dillon informed Mrs. Champlin about her opportunities for service at Urban Day and her related obligation to maintain Michelle's attendance. She was carefully apprised of the fact that if she did not maintain regular attendance for her daughter that services for Michelle would be terminated. Mrs. Champlin stated firmly that she preferred termination. So the case was closed by Urban Day. Mrs. Champlin was given a list of potential resources to consult in the future and was also invited to contact Urban Day if she wished to commence service once more. Blue County Protective Services was advised by Urban Day of the termination of the center's involvement with the Champlin family.

Termination was a sad time for the Urban Day staff because they knew they were the agency of last resort. No other agency would step in to advocate for Michelle unless she suffered crisis-level abuse in the future. But Urban Day had done everything it could do and had left its doors open for further service if requested.

Further Considerations

To conclude the discussion of the ethical principle relating to primacy of clients' interests, let us briefly examine provisions two, four, and five, which have been neglected so far. Provision two reads: "The social worker should not exploit relationships with clients for personal advantage, or solicit the clients of one's agency for private practice." This consideration refers primarily to social workers with salaried agency jobs who also have a private practice on the side. It is unethical to draw clients from one's agency work into one's private practice for personal monetary profit. To avoid conflicts of interest, if agency clients need more intensive counseling than can be provided in that setting, the soical worker should refer the clients elsewhere.

Provision four reads: "The social worker should avoid relationships or commitments that conflict with the interests of the clients." A possible example from Urban Day might be if a worker were to become so emotionally involved with the needs of a parent that the needs of the child might be overlooked. Great care is taken to avoid this circumstance, as will be illustrated later in this chapter. Of course, this provision might also refer to a quite different set of circumstances, instructing the social worker to avoid close personal ties with other professionals who might have power over the same set of clients to avoid conflicts of interest.

Provision five states: "The social worker should under no circumstance engage in sexual activities with clients." This ethical assertion arises out of some years of debate. At one time certain professionals believed that sexual activity might enhance the self-image of clients, make them feel more special and loved. However, new insights into sexual activity as a relationship of power rather than love (under certain circumstances) renders inclusion of this provision in the code very important. Clients can too easily be manipulated into sexual activity hoping that compliance will bring them marital rights, or at least special favors. They can later be devastated to learn that the sexual activity was not a symbol of love by the professional but just for the client's own good, with no further intentions. On the other hand, it might be perfectly possible for a professional to be talked into sexual activity by a client, only to have this information used for power purposes later by the client as a kind of blackmail. Sexual activity is just too multiple in its meanings and consequences to be worth the risk.

RIGHTS AND PREROGATIVES OF CLIENTS

The second principle of the social worker's ethical responsibility to clients involves the right of clients to make their own decisions, or to use the language of the code of ethics: "The social worker should make every effort to foster self-determination on the part of clients."

Self-determination for clients is a value which has long held a venerated place in the professional social work value system. What self-determination is all about is the concept that clients should be able to make the final decisions regarding what they do for themselves or have others do for them. Social workers can identify options for clients which the clients may not have thought of at first, and can help the client explore the merits or limitations of any and all options. Social workers may even give their best professional opinion regarding their own preferred choice of option, particularly if that opinion is voluntarily sought. However, the final decision must remain with the client.

Implementing this value as part of practice ethics can be surprisingly difficult. For one thing, it makes intuitive sense to realize that a client may continue to make decisions that are distressing to the social worker and which may seem essentially self-destructive (e.g., remaining in a living situation involving severe physical abuse). At Urban Day, however, and by extension any agency dealing with children, there is another type of major problem. The client system is two-tiered, to speak metaphorically. The set of clients around which the services of the agency are oriented are minor children who do not have the legal right to make the major decisions that will affect them. And there is also a set of clients related to the agency only through the children, the parents, legal guardians, or others, who have the legal right to make all the major decisions for the children.

Who has the right to self-determine when the primary client is a handicapped child? Suppose, as has already been illustrated in previous sections, the best professional opinion of the social worker in terms of what should be done for a given child differs radically from the wishes of the parents. Suppose that in the social worker's best professional assessment, the choices preferred by the parents could be literally physically destructive for the child. Such cases do arise at Urban Day.

In some, as in the case of Michelle, there is no real choice. The parent has the legal right to decide about services regarding the child, and that is final. In extremely abusive situations the courts can be brought in through the intervention of a public protective services department, which can advocate for a transfer of custody or legal guardianship and foster home placement. This is what happened with Cora Evans and her twins for a short while. A private, voluntary agency like Urban Day can only refer the case to protective services and hope. In fact, then, the adult client with full legal rights has self-determination not because self-determination is a social work value, but because it is the law in the United States. The voluntary client who insists on self-determination has the legal right to do so.

In the case of the adult client without dependents, even in situations where the client chooses self-destructive courses of action against the advice of the social worker, protecting that right of choice should be of vital concern to the social worker. None of us as free citizens would want to lose the right to make our own choices, not even if people with wiser heads would urge us to make different choices, be they friends, parents, colleagues, or counselors. In fact, reflecting the importance of personal freedom and self-determination, the third provision of the code of ethics under the rights and prerogatives of clients principle states clearly that "the social worker should not engage in any action that violates or diminishes the civil or legal rights of clients."

But again, what if the primary client of the social worker is a minor child, and according to the professional assessment of the social worker the parent seems to be making destructive choices for that child? What then? Then it behooves the social worker to do whatever is possible on behalf of that child within the limits of the law. The relevant guideline of the code of ethics is the second provision under the rights and prerogatives of clients principle: "When another individual has been legally authorized to act in behalf of a client, the social worker should deal with that person always with the client's best interests in mind." This provision might apply to adults who have been adjudicated incompetent, and a guardian may be appointed in their behalf by the courts, although provision one applies specifically to such persons. It can also apply to children, whose parents are legally authorized by society to act in their behalf. But if parents have the legal right to make the major choices for their children, regardless of Urban Day's professional assessment of the advisability of their choices, what can the staff do for the children?

The social worker's interpersonal skills can often be effectively mobilized in ways that influence parents to change dramatically and voluntarily, at least as far as outlook on special services for their children is concerned. Thus, a major function of the Urban Day social services staff is to enable parents to permit Urban Day to work with their children. Strongly motivated to work in behalf of the children and respecting the rights and basic good intentions of most parents, the social service staff can in most cases gradually influence the parents to permit their children to receive services. The roles so frequently listed in methods texts are all used, for example, educating, informing, mobilizing, supporting, enabling, influencing, brokering, advocating, coordinating, and mediating (badgering, handholding, etc.). That particular role related to support called caring is often involved in reaching the most difficult parents, though the caring must be kept in careful bounds because of the excessive demands it can create.

Let's examine a case where the ethical principle of self-determination for clients clearly worked and could be applied in pure form. Daryl Knopps was referred to Urban Day by the Central Referral Committee because of extensive epileptic seizures. Daryl was almost two years old when he was referred, but he still couldn't walk. However, he was an extremely active little boy and seemed to be frustrated by his inability to move around with any degree of coordination. Daryl tended to throw himself about in all directions and so had to wear a football helmet at all times to prevent serious head injury, as he banged into anything or anyone that got near him. His sight came and went, although the doctors couldn't diagnose why. His behavior was particularly wild during his blind episodes. Daryl needed several services: physical therapy to help develop coordination in his larger body muscles; speech therapy because his main means of communication was a constant, inarticulate sort of roaring sound; and continuous attention because of his highly distractable behavior. He was also on constant medication which wasn't working as it should to calm his behavior and his seizures, so he needed medical monitoring by the Urban Day nurse in consultation with his doctors.

As is probably evident from this behavioral description, Daryl did not provide his parents many rewards for parenthood. He was constantly on the move, roaring inarticulately, heaving into furniture and people. He used a walker but was continually throwing himself out of it. His mother was literally exhausted from the child-care demands. She had another child, a normal little girl, whom she worried she was neglecting due to the demands from Daryl. Daryl's parents had a strong, intact marriage which provided them with emotional support, yet they were extremely grateful to Urban Day for the relief from constant pressure created by Daryl's presence in the home, and grateful for a setting in which they could discuss their children and their child-related problems.

Once Daryl was referred to Urban Day, the parents demonstrated that they were thoughtful, discriminating consumers of service opportunities. They first asked relevant questions regarding the services available at Urban Day and then asked to make an appointment to tour the center. Once they learned what was available they became responsible, appreciative clients. They knew what they wanted for their son and asked about other potential resources, both within and outside of Urban Day. The role of the social service staff could essentially be educational and supportive. If the Knopps had questions, they asked. If they were upset or overwhelmed due to current problems, they talked about what was bothering them. They did not swallow Mrs. Haley's suggestions whole, but considered them and accepted what fit for them. This family chose to enroll Daryl at Urban Day and maintained frequent contact. They maintained Daryl's attendance regularly except on days when the little boy was actually sick. Then, when the boy was old enough to leave Urban Day, they chose to enroll him in full-day programming elsewhere, both because they felt he needed extensive treatment for himself and because the family as a whole could cope so much better with the boy at home only early mornings and evenings. The public school would not fund full-day programming for Daryl due to budget cuts, so the family enrolled him in a private program dealing with older children for the other half day. Mrs. Haley had told them she doubted the little boy would be able to cope with adjusting to two different new programs at the same time, but according to the principle of self-determination, the parents made their own decision. However, they returned for more consultation when the new plan indeed did not work.

It is very common at Urban Day for former clients to return from time to time, to renew meaningful contacts or to discuss new problems. Mrs. Haley encouraged the Knopps to discuss their current problem in detail. After sorting through the behavioral difficulties Daryl was exhibiting in his new programs and potential causes and solutions, the parents decided to enroll Daryl full-time in the private program, even though that would cost them considerably more money. That option would provide the child with more consistent care and behavioral monitoring. So far, this decision is working.

The Knopps case history is an example of a circumstance in which self-determination worked well, not only in principle but in practice. Of course, it helped that the family had enough income to finance their choices. The following story is an illustration of a different situation in which the principle of self-determination involved some powerful challenges for the Urban Day staff.

The Johnston Case

The Johnston case has already been introduced in the previous chapter. Little Bobbie and his older sister Luann were both afflicted by severe cases of cerebral palsy, and their twenty-one-year-old mother often failed to send them to school. The efforts of Urban Day's community worker, Mrs. Dillon, to persuade the mother to send them more regularly were unsuccessful. This circumstance weighed on Mrs. Dillon heavily, because Bobbie and Luann were children who badly needed the services Urban Day had to offer, and who visibly improved in their physical mobility and speech patterns when they did attend the center. Under no conditions did Mrs. Dillon want to give up on these children, but she knew she might have to. One possibility would be for her to get Blue County Protective Services involved, but this was not a clear case of child abuse. She suspected the workers would simply visit the home once or twice and encourage the mother to maintain attendance at Urban Day. That would be all they could do. Ms. Johnston had the legal right to keep her children with her during the day, if that is what she preferred.

This was a time when Urban Day had plenty of referrals and had a waiting list. Other children were being denied service to hold the place for the Johnston children. Their unmet needs also weighed on Mrs. Dillon. Had she a right to hold a place for Bobbie and Luann if they were not attending very regularly, whereas other children might come in every day as scheduled?

She consulted with Mrs. Haley. Together the social services director and the community worker explored the possible options. As with the Champlin case, they could drop the Johnston children from the program and justify the move with the waiting list. But that would probably cost both children their chance for future mobility and undo all the work Urban Day had already invested in them. Mrs. Haley supported Mrs. Dillon in her desire to continue trying to work with this family. She suggested that Mrs. Dillon go to the home in person again, this time specifically to inform Ms. Johnston that regular attendance was a requirement of service and to gain some sense from the mother if termination was really what she wanted. If so, there would not be much Urban Day could do, except threaten a protective services referral. That might motivate Ms. Johnston to comply for a while, because she would not know at first that such a threat would be relatively empty. The decision was made not to involve protective services at this time, but rather to identify family strengths that might be mobilized to assist in getting the children to the center. Also, were there any particular circumstances going on with Ms. Johnston lately that were interfering with the children's attendance at the center? After all, in the very beginning the attendance had been regular by comparison, even if never exemplary.

Mrs. Dillon scheduled a long afternoon with Ms. Johnston in order to have plenty of time to talk with the young mother at her own pace. She conducted a low-key conversation with Ms. Johnston that flowed more like an afternoon coffee klatch between neighbors than a worker–client interview. Nevertheless, Mrs. Dillon was clear about her objectives and knew that she could meet them only if her client could begin to trust her as a human being. Ms. Johnston gradually relaxed after some period of time. She began to share her feelings, hesitantly at first, and then more openly. She knew her children needed help, she explained, she really did. She was glad that the center was offering her children service; it was just that sometimes, the bus came so very early in the morning. Ms. Johnston wanted to have the children ready on time but sometimes she just couldn't wake up. She was sorry; she would try to do better in the future. But then—and the twenty-one-year-old mother of two looked at her feet as her eyes filled with tears—sometimes the days were so long without the children home. Her mother didn't drop by so much and she got so lonely. She had so many personal problems now. The children's father, whom she loved and wanted, and who used to visit sometimes, had gone back down south only last month and planned to stay there. He couldn't get a job in Project City. He hadn't written since he left. Ms. Johnston cried and said she just felt so alone. She had felt so upset when both children were born handicapped. She was afraid that might be the real reason her boyfriend had finally left her.

The boyfriend who had recently left her was the father of both children. The children had been planned, and both parents had looked forward to their birth. The cerebral palsy had been caused during the birth process of both children—the umbilical chord had wrapped around their necks and cut off the oxygen supply for a critical period of time. The father had been good to Ms. Johnston for quite some time after the two births (a year apart) and had even helped with child care at times, but he just wasn't proud of Bobbie and Luann and seemed to lose interest over time.

As a result of this conversation, Mrs. Dillon felt clearly that Ms. Johnston was indeed interested in her children and their care, but that she herself was so depressed and lonely that she couldn't function as she wanted. Mrs. Dillon also learned that her client had several resources that she might be able to mobilize in working with the young mother. For one thing, she discovered that Ms. Johnston had a close personal relationship with her concerned mother. Perhaps Ms. Johnston's mother could help in some way. She had an adult brother in town as well, who might be drawn in to help at times. Mrs. Dillon also learned that Ms. Johnston did want her children to receive treatment at Urban Day. She was failing to cooperate not because she didn't want the service, but because her own life was in a shambles. The young mother's emotional depression and inability to get up in the morning seemed to be interfering with her goals for her children. But the depression was precipitated by a genuine loss. Any young woman would be depressed and downhearted by the loss of a boyfriend, especially the father of her two children. Perhaps the present situation could be restructured in some way to give the mother needed support through this difficult period in her life.

Mrs. Dillon began her course of action with an immediate and practical plan as to how to help Ms. Johnston wake up in the morning. As she suspected from the tone of the mother's voice on the phone in the morning, Ms. Johnston said she did not like to be awakened with a telephone call. She wanted to wake herself up or not at all. Mrs. Dillon asked if she had an alarm clock. She did not. Mrs. Dillon suggested that the two of them might go out and purchase one at the local dime store. That was acceptable to Ms. Johnston, so the two women had a pleasant shopping trip together. In this way, Mrs. Dillon was already injecting a new source of support into Ms. Johnston's life—herself. By the time she left the young mother at her apartment again, she had been assured that the two children would be on the bus the next morning.

And they were. Mrs. Dillon called to thank Ms. Johnston sincerely. That worked for about a week. Then the children stopped coming again. Mrs. Dillon called, to find that the telephone had been disconnected. She decided to call Ms. Johnston's mother. Perhaps the children's grandmother might know where they were, and might have some ideas as to how to encourage their mother to get them to come to school. When Mrs. Dillon reached the grandmother on the telephone, she found that she had an ally. The grandmother was clearly concerned about the welfare of Bobbie and Luann and said that she talked with their mother frequently about the importance of getting the children to school. Ms. Dillon decided to go out to the grandmother's home to meet with her in person, because she thought perhaps the woman might have new ideas regarding how to work most effectively with Ms. Johnston. The grandmother, Mrs. Simpson, turned out to feel stymied as well, however. "Do what you can with my daughter," the grandmother begged Mrs. Dillon. "I try, I try as hard as I can but sometimes she just won't listen."

Mrs. Dillon then remembered that Ms. Johnston had mentioned that her mother didn't drop by to see her as often when Bobbie and Luann were at school. She realized from meeting the grandmother that she was a supportive person whose attention might be important in alleviating Ms. Johnston's depression. However, she had three fairly young children, Ms. Johnston's half siblings, living with her, ranging from four through eleven years of age. Certainly they would require a lot of time and attention from Mrs. Simpson, too, detracting from what she could offer Ms. Johnston.

Mrs. Dillon had an idea. Perhaps Mrs. Simpson could encourage her daughter, Ms. Johnston, to come over and spend many of her daytime hours with her, while Bobbie and Luann were at school. Ms. Johnston could then help care for her half brothers and sisters, and receive needed attention for herself in this way. Perhaps then she would receive the support she needed in getting Bobbie and Luann off to Urban Day in the morning.

Mrs. Simpson agreed. While she said Ms. Johnston knew she was welcome to come over to her house any time already, she thought that making a special invitation might help. She agreed to talk to her daughter about spending more time with her that day. With this kind of support system available, Mrs. Dillon felt hopeful that she would be able to help work out some kind of arrangement that would get Bobbie and Luann to Urban Day on a regular basis. Her next step was to talk with Ms. Johnston again. She found the young mother at home; the telephone had been disconnected due to nonpayment of the bill. Ms. Johnston was extremely depressed. Owing to her financial worries and her depression, she had had too much to drink the night before and had slept through the alarm clock. She felt tired, apologetic, discouraged, and sick. She was tired of failing. She told Mrs. Dillon that she thought it was time to withdraw her children from Urban Day. She was just too exhausted to get up every morning to get Bobbie and Luann ready for the bus, and she couldn't imagine ever feeling otherwise.

Mrs. Dillon realized that the relationship between herself and the young woman had approached a crisis point. If she gave up on Ms. Johnston now, the mother would simply feel relieved, and that would be that. If she antagonized Ms. Johnston through reprimanding her for irresponsible behavior, the mother would withdraw completely. All Mrs. Dillon had to go on, in extending the possibility for Bobbie and Luann to attend school, was her relationship with Ms. Johnston, her interpersonal skills, and her commitment to her profession and the handicapped children themselves. Of course, she also had Mrs. Simpson, the grandmother.

Mrs. Dillon decided she had identified enough strengths in this family situation to persist. Ms. Johnston was young and had a whole life ahead of her. She had a supportive mother. The young woman had basically good intentions. She was just thoroughly depressed. Mrs. Dillon decided to call Mrs. Simpson to find out if care for Bobbie and Luann could be informally shifted for a while. And perhaps if Ms. Johnston could live with Mrs. Simpson for short time as well, her depression might lift.

Mrs. Simpson came over to talk with her daughter and Mrs. Dillon together, bringing her youngest child in tow. She was willing to do whatever was wanted or needed. Ms. Johnston decided she wanted to remain in her own apartment, but she was grateful to have the responsibility for Bobbie and Luann taken off her hands for a while. She decided to send them over to live with their grandmother for a few days while she sorted out her personal problems. Both of the older women worried about Ms. Johnston staying in her apartment alone, but they received a promise from her that she would talk to Mrs. Simpson or visit Urban Day if she felt the need. Mrs. Simpson also called the girl's brother and his wife to ask them to visit Ms. Johnston frequently during the next couple of weeks.

This story could go on and on. In fact, it did, for the ensuing two years when both children were served by Urban Day at first, and then just one, as the oldest, Luann, went on to the public schools. To make a long story short, at times Bobbie and Luann were cared for by their grandmother; at times they went home with their mother. At times the alarm clock worked for Ms. Johnston; at times even a telephone call wasn't enough or the telephone was disconnected. At those times the grandmother, Mrs. Dillon, or even a neighbor went over to the mother's house early in the morning to wake her up. A combination of a basic desire for service for her children on the part of Ms. Johnston, the patience of her neighbors, family, and friends, and an intense professional and personal commitment on the part of Mrs. Dillon and other Urban Day staff made service for Bobbie and Luann a reality. Several approaches were used. While it was clear Ms. Johnston cared about her children and wanted them to receive services for that reason, and her depression was the primary reason she failed, she also made some immature decisions and needed confrontation at times. For example, sometimes she didn't get up in the morning not because of depression but because of normal fatigue—she had stayed up all night carousing with her brother and his family!

At least once a protective services referral was threatened, and once the children were actually terminated at Urban Day for a few weeks. Termination was a calculated risk, of course. When, after a period of marked improvement, the children's attendance fell off drastically again, Mrs. Dillon tried reinstating the telephone call procedure and it didn't work. Mrs. Dillon, in consultation with Mrs. Haley, then decided that termination would in this case probably mobilize the mother's own energies toward meeting requirements that were clear to her. As expected, shortly after termination of service at Urban Day, Ms. Johnston came in to the center in person to ask for her children's reinstatement. Her voluntary request provided an effective opportunity to clarify with her why she wanted treatment for Bobbie and Luann. Ms. Johnston was able to sort out her own emotional needs from the physical needs of her children, and she agreed to develop an individual contract with Mrs. Dillon where she was required to get the children to the center a certain number of days each week in order for them to remain in the program.

Eventually, Ms. Johnston recovered from her depression. Part of the trick was that she began to respond to the attention from the professionals working with her, her children, and her family. Also, she met a somewhat older man who took an interest in her and treated her in an appreciative, caring way. Ms. Johnston's self-esteem went up through all these sources of attention. Her behavior became increasingly self-directed and responsible. By the time Bobbie left Urban Day at the age of three, his attendance record was almost normal. So was Luann's at the public school program, where Bobbie would go next. Both children had made enormous gains.

How does the principle of self-determination relate to this case?

Bobbie and Luann received treatement at Urban Day, and later at the public schools, because basically that is what their mother wanted. Enabling Ms. Johnston to achieve her real wants, however, despite a good deal of contrary behavior, required an enormous investment of effort on the part of many people besides herself. Self-determination for Ms. Johnston was a product of the interaction among a number of systems other than (and including) her own person. It involved much larger national and state social policy options which provided special education funding for handicapped children which other people developed and fought for. It involved Urban Day's overall agency policy which provided a social service staff as well as teachers and therapists. It involved a relationship with a caring social worker. In addition, it involved extended family efforts, and later the input of a new boyfriend, as well as other less obvious factors. Yet without basic self-determination, all the interactional factors from the other systems wouldn't have resulted in treatment for Bobbie and Luann, as has been illustrated earlier in the case of Michele Champlin. Self-determination is a complex concept!

The Jenkins Case

The case of Richard Jenkins is another example in which the Urban Day staff made enormous efforts in order to enable self-determination on the part of a parent. Richard, actually Richard Jr., was burned terribly in a household fire when he was just a little over a year old. He received third-degree burns over fifty percent of his body. That he lived at all is somewhat of a miracle. He spent about four months in intensive care in an excellent Project City hospital known for its expertise in working with burn victims. The hospital social service staff referred Richard to Urban Day before releasing him because extensive physical, occupational, and speech therapy would be needed. Richard would require extensive skin grafting and plastic surgery in the future. Most of his fingers and toes had been burned away but a few parts remained that might be taught to grasp and function in basic ways. His face had been burned to such a degree that extensive therapy would be required to teach him to use his mouth effectively for speaking. Richard, in short, would need ongoing help from both the hospital and the Urban Day program or he would never be able to care for himself or communicate normally.

When Mrs. Haley first received Richard's referral, she was concerned because none of the staff at Urban Day had experience working with burned children. Her concern led her to read about the needs and problems of burn victims. She arranged to have the hospital where Richard was treated put on an in-service training workshop for the entire Urban Day staff. This accomplished, the staff felt more prepared to work with Richard Jr.

When the boy first arrived he was obviously in pain. He cried all the time, moved his body around constantly, and wouldn't eat. Salve had to be applied frequently for itching; his healing skin was tender and oozing all over his body. Naturally, the staff was concerned when he missed the bus twice the first week. Mrs. Haley, who decided to work with this case herself, contacted the mother, Amanda Jenkins, to find out more about her situation. A strikingly beautiful young black woman, Ms. Jenkins was single, only nineteen years old, and trying to cope on her own with myriad problems. Perhaps her largest immediate problem was money. Her public assistance grant had not been sufficient to pay all her bills that month, her utilities had been turned off, and she was living alone in an apartment in late autumn without heat, hot water, or electricity with a little burn victim who had just been released from the hospital. Mrs. Haley arranged immediately to find temporary housing at an emergency shelter for the two of them.

She began to discuss options with Amanda Jenkins. Was there anyone from whom she could borrow money to get her utilities turned back on? The only immediate possibility turned out to be the child's father, Richard Sr., with whom she had been involved for years. Like many poor, inner-city couples the two young adults had never married because that would disqualify the family from Aid to Families with Dependent Children and Medicaid. Richard Sr. frequently worked but his job insecurity was such that marriage was considered too risky. In the times when Richard Sr. was out of work, the family would have no income to carry them through the hard times. Certainly if the two had been married when Richard Jr. was burned in the fire, the family would have been wiped out by medical bills, whether the father had a job or not. Most inner-city jobs pay poorly and carry no insurance benefits. The state in which Urban Day Center is located does have a program called Aid to Families of Dependent Children—Unemployed Parent, an optional program under the provisions of the Social Security Act and carried by only half the states. This program is designed to help intact families whose adult members are usually employed get through temporary bouts of extended unemployment. Few families, however, actually qualify for this aid. The father must have worked a certain number of months in a qualifying job in the immediate past, and inner city men often can't meet the requirement. An unmarried couple is economically safer in the inner city—at least the mother and the children can count on a steady, though poverty-level, income.

Nonetheless, this was a time when Amanda might have been able to borrow from Richard Sr. He had been working for a few months. But she did not want to contact him. Amanda explained to Mrs. Haley that sometimes he beat her up, and she did not want to be in debt to him. He might take it out on her later. Moreover, as Mrs. Haley talked with the nineteen-year-old mother, it became obvious she was overwhelmed by the responsibility of caring for her baby. He really was frightening to look at at this time and required enormous amounts of physical care. Providing for Richard Jr.'s needs seemed impossibly difficult for the young mother. To make matters more difficult, Amanda herself was afflicted with epileptic seizures on occasion, for which she received a small monthly disability stipend. Stress tended to trigger the seizures. She was frightened. She asked Mrs. Haley if it would be possible to place Richard Jr. in a foster home for a while. Mrs. Haley checked with Blue County Department of Public Welfare and found that a placement was available. That seemed appropriate to all involved, until such time as Ms. Jenkins could pull herself together and have her heat and utilities turned back on. By then, too, perhaps little Richard's condition would improve.

While Richard Jr. was in foster care, he attended Urban Day regularly. Mrs. Haley got to know Amanda Jenkins well because she came to the center frequently to observe her little boy. Mrs. Haley worked with Amanda to teach her the stages of normal child development and the possible effects of the burns. She found in Amanda a likeable, frightened girl who had had some hard knocks in her life. Literally. Mrs. Haley helped Amanda talk about her experiences with physical abuse from the child's father. She talked with her about the possibility of ending that relationship. But Amanda felt that despite the abuse, she loved Richard Sr. One day she brought him in to Urban Day Center to observe Richard Jr. in the playroom. She seemed proud of her son and the father that day. Mrs. Haley had a long talk with the young father about Richard Jr. He was attentive and polite, and asked questions that indicated real concern. Like most battering men, he was not a monster under normal circumstances. After that initial visit, Richard Sr. occasionally came to Urban Day by himself to observe his son and talk to Mrs. Haley about his progress.

After a few weeks, Richard seemed to be doing much better physically. Amanda felt ready to bring him home. Mrs. Haley felt she would be able to care for the child. She helped Ms. Jenkins reestablish the Aid to Families with Dependent Children grant for Richard Jr., and she negotiated the boy's return home with the foster-care workers. Somewhere in that process, Ms. Jenkins managed to scrape up the money required to get her utilities turned back on. And so Richard Jr. came home.

What followed was a saga much like that of the Johnston family. Although well-intentioned, Ms. Jenkins often did not get Richard Jr. to school in the morning. The staff would have to go out and transport the child. Sometimes telephone calls worked and sometimes they didn't. Occasionally when Amanda Jenkins missed putting the child on the bus, she would bring the boy in herself, apologizing profusely. She meant well, but her life was often out of control. Sometimes her boyfriend would come over and they would get into a fight. The next morning the young mother would be too upset to get Richard Jr. on the bus. Throughout it all, however, Mrs. Haley worked with her persistently, encouraging her, chiding her, believing in her. Mrs. Haley also encouraged the young father, or the

couple together, to seek counseling, but Richard Sr. refused.
Finally, when Richard Jr.'s attendance didn't stabilize, Mrs. Haley assigned Emily Gantz, a forthright, no-nonsense member of the social service staff, to work on the case with her. At this time, Emily was working on a special grant which permitted training of selected parents to work with their children in the home. Ms. Jenkins seemed like an ideal candidate for this training. It would hopefully teach her more about Richard's special needs and how to work with them and sensitize her to his need for regular therapy at Urban Day. In this way Emily also became directly involved in social service intervention with the Jenkins family.

Emily Gantz and Mrs. Haley began to share responsibility for the Jenkins case. Mrs. Haley provided most of the day-to-day intervention to help improve attendance, and Mrs. Gantz taught Amanda basic child development skills for use in the home. Shortly after beginning their work, the two women decided to make a home visit together, on a day when little Richard didn't arrive at Urban Day on the bus. Mrs. Haley and Emily decided to confront the mother together for effect. Upon their arrival, however, they found that Amanda had been badly beaten the night before. In fact, she had been beaten so badly that she had jumped out of her second-story window to avoid a fate that seemed worse at the time. Richard Sr. had then fortunately left. Amanda's foot was broken in the fall, and she was scratched and bruised from the fight. Crawling back up the stairs had exhausted and infuriated her. This time, she was persuaded to file a legal complaint against her boyfriend.

She was sobbing hysterically, so both women took her to the district attorney's office, one doing the driving and one carrying Richard Jr. and attempting to calm Amanda. After what seemed to be a great deal of time and confusion, the legal complaint was filed. Everybody returned to Ms. Jenkins's apartment, with the intention of talking through her remaining anxieties. Unexpectedly, however, Richard Sr. was waiting at the apartment. He was drunk. He made a few inflammatory comments to Amanda as she entered the door, and before either of the Urban Day staff could intervene, Amanda shouted back some equally unflattering phrases. Richard Sr. then leaped bodily at Amanda, who grabbed whatever objects were near at hand and began to throw them. It all happened very fast.

At this juncture, Mrs. Haley's basic faith in both people, whom she felt she knew well, came to the fore. She fully believed that neither Richard nor Amanda would hurt her personally, at least not intentionally. So she thrust her five-foot, ninety-eight-pound body between the furious pair. This type of sacrificial act is not required by the code of ethics! However, Mrs. Haley trusted her judgment that neither combatant would hurt her personally, and she feared for Amanda Jenkin's life, as Richard was a big man.

So she thrust herself between them, and fortunately, she was right. Her physical intervention between the enraged parents kept them apart. However, they did not totally stop their fighting. Richard Sr. kept trying to reach Amanda around the edges and over the top of Mrs. Haley, and Amanda kept trying to slug her boyfriend however she could. Mrs. Gantz, recognizing a temporary stalemate, ran down the stairs of the apartment building with Richard Jr. in her arms, roused a neighbor, called the police, and was able to persuade the neighbor to come quickly to help. The neighbor, who knew both people involved, miraculously came to the rescue. Since Richard Sr. was drunk and the neighbor was not, he was able to get the angry boyfriend to the door. The young father rushed out furiously. The police came much later, and another complaint was filed.

One would like to be able to report that shortly thereafter, Amanda Jenkins actually broke up with her boyfriend. She didn't. She did not feel capable of carrying on by herself without a man. Any man was better than none in her value system. According to her self-concept, a woman without a man was worthless. So she made up with Richard Sr. again, withdrew the legal charges, and things went on as before. Care for Richard Jr. continued to fluctuate abysmally, and attendance at Urban Day fluctuated as well. Emily Gantz finally confronted Mrs. Haley. "I think we ought to refer Amanda Jenkins to protective services," Mrs. Gantz said in her straightforward way. "You like this woman too much, and that's why you don't see things the way I see them. The way I see things, Amanda's not going to do one thing to change her life unless protective services takes that child away. It's not fair to the child to leave him with her. Richard Jr.'s not getting the care he needs for those burns. Protective services will take him away from her, too, if we testify in court, because he needs so much medical care that he's not getting."

"But Emily," Mrs. Haley objected. "Amanda's doing all right; considering the circumstances, she's doing the best she can. She'd fall apart now if we took that child away from her. Sure his attendance isn't regular here, but she's taking pretty good care of him at home now. He's her only reason for living just now, and she loves him. I think the best chance for both of them to make it in life is to stay together."

Mrs. Haley, as supervisor, had the strongest say in this kind of decision. Emily had the legal right to make a complaint on her own, of course, but without the backing of her supervisor, it would be difficult to put her whole self into it. Being human, she might worry about keeping her position, though Mrs. Haley would never penalize a worker for doing a responsible job. But Mrs. Haley didn't want to proceed with a legal complaint. She felt strongly that Amanda was making progress, and that the progress could be jeopardized if Amanda lost her trust in her primary social worker, Mrs. Haley.

This is one example of what the fourth provision under the primacy of clients' interests principle of the second category of the code of ethics dealing with ethical responsibility to clients is warning about. Provision four, as noted previously, states as follows: "The social worker should avoid relationships or commitments that conflict with the interests of the clients." Here is a circumstance in which Mrs. Haley, in working with the parent, Amanda Jenkins, with "devotion, loyalty, and determination" may have developed *too* much loyalty to the young mother in order to generate the energy to keep going with this difficult case. The nature of some cases may put practitioners in a double blind—in order to serve a given client loyally despite seemingly insurmountable odds, social workers may have to commit themselves to the client in a way that can blind them to the client's limitations. This is one reason why consultation and supervision is so strongly recommended for social workers, so that they will have access to other perspectives. At any rate, from Emily Gantz' perspective at least, the time came when Mrs. Haley's commitment to Amanda Jenkins may have conflicted with the best interests of the primary client, Richard Jr. What happened next is an example of creative problem solving that can only arise in circumstances of respect and forthright communication between supervisor and staff.

In the midst of disagreeing with Mrs. Gantz, Mrs. Haley remembered a tactic she had learned when, prior to her enrollment in graduate school, she had been a policewoman. The tactic she recalled was used to elicit confessions from suspected criminals. The suspect would be interviewed by a team of two. One member of the team would be the bad guy, mean and awful. After that member gave the suspect a terrible time verbally, the other member of the team would speak up gently and sympathetically, and come across as a friend. The suspect would trust the good intentions of the sympathetic policeman and was likely to tell a great deal. Later, the suspect would learn that too much had been told! To heighten the effect of this tactic, the police would unsettle the suspect further by having the person originally expected to be sympathetic be the bad guy, for example, a petite, attractive young woman. The sympathetic role would be played by a big, tough-looking male. Mrs. Haley, of course, got to play the "bad guy" role most of the time. She hated it. They told her she ought to be a social worker, and not in a very complimentary fashion! She went on to do just that.

Now Mrs. Haley made creative use of her police training. She recognized that *both* clients—little Richard Jr. *and* his mother Amanda— needed advocacy in their best interests. Moreover, in order to meet the needs of little Richard, his mother was going to have to make some changes in her life. As suggested by Emily Gantz, supportive and educational tactics might not be enough to bring about the needed changes. Perhaps, since the needs of the two clients were different, the same advocate could not equally well represent both, and the advocate for the son could take on a confrontational role with the mother. So Mrs. Haley had a brainstorm. She asked Mrs. Gantz to represent Richard in the best and strongest way she knew how. She, Mrs. Haley, would not interfere. However, Mrs. Haley would advocate for Amanda's best interests. That way, if Emily wanted to file a protective services complaint on Richard Jr.'s behalf, she could provide the needed confrontational role in changing Amanda's behavior. Mrs. Haley would support the mother and continue to work with her using positive means to modify her parenting behavior.

Most social work agencies assign a single staff member to work with a given family. This is often a good idea in that it allows the staff member to assess and work with the needs of the family as a whole. On the other hand, the disadvantage is that one worker often cannot advocate equally effectively for children and parents when their perceived needs are different. By dividing responsibility for working with different members of the same family, Urban Day could assign an advocate for Richard Jr. and a different advocate for the mother. The clarity of roles hopefully would offset the difficulties encountered by the two staff members sometimes working at cross puposes. The respect each held for the other, and their ability to understand one another's point of view, would facilitate cordial collegial relations.

As Mrs. Haley suspected, she and Emily did not work at cross purposes. In her role as Richard's Jr.'s advocate, Emily could, through filing and diligently following up on her protective services complaint, actually assist Mrs. Haley in her own work with Amanda Jenkins. This could be so because Mrs. Gantz was honest with Amanda and explained to her clearly that (1) she was initiating a formal complaint and (2) her reasons for doing so. Because Mrs. Gantz believed so firmly in what she was doing, Amanda got the message that her continued custody of her son was in jeopardy. On the other hand, Amanda trusted in Mrs. Haley's own equally honest message to her—that she was doing well in her basic mothering and was a worthwhile person—but she did need to make changes in her child-care behaviors, including maintaining Richard Jr.'s attendance at Urban Day. She also needed to maintain his medical appointments and treatment more regularly.

Mrs. Gantz pressed the protective services case into an advanced stage where the case was actually in court and a guardian *ad litum*, or court-appointed attorney to protect the needs of the child, was assigned. The outcome of the case was uncertain for a while. But with her fear of losing custody of Richard Jr. (the result of Mrs. Gantz's efforts) and the steady support and coaching provided by Mrs. Haley, Amanda Jenkins changed.

At the time of this writing, Richard Jr. is still living at home with his mother and is nearing the age of three. His physical condition is so much improved that his exit plan is expected to involve normal day care only, with outpatient therapy from Urban Day. He can walk almost normally, use his hands effectively though to a limited degree, and feed himself with a spoon equipped with a special device designed to help him hold it. His first move when he sees any of the social service staff is to walk up proudly and give them a kiss. He talks happily and clearly and is at the appropriate age level intellectually.

His life will probably not be easy. The disfigurement of his face remains despite extensive skin grafting. Mrs. Haley reports going with his mother to a medical appointment lately to see a new doctor. The physician took one look at little Richard and exclaimed loudly, "My God, what happened to that kid?" Richard, who looks too little and disfigured to understand much, is sensitive and understands just about everything. His face fell and he slumped all over. He'll need ongoing positive input from people who know and love him to make his life worthwhile, which is why it is so nice he has been able to remain with his natural mother.

Mrs. Gantz said to the writer of this book, "Well, I guess on hindsight I was wrong. Amanda Jenkins really did shape up. She really did learn to maintain Richard Jr.'s attendance and keep his medical appointments." Mrs. Haley, on another occasion, said, "Well, I guess Emily was right. I don't think without the threat of protective services that things would have worked out this well at all."

Amanda Jenkins is a familiar sight at Urban Day as this chapter is being written. She studies frequently for her GED (high school equivalency diploma) in the agency lounge. Mrs. Haley is realistic. "We'll be seeing her for a long time after Richard has been discharged. She gets a lot of her self-esteem from this place. She's still seeing the same boyfriend and probably will continue to do so, but at least she knows now she's not completely worthless without him. Her self-concept isn't totally tied up in that relationship any more. She wants to go on to get her GED and then get a job, and I'm encouraging her all I can, but sometimes I wonder. I know she's doing this mostly to please us. Will there be any payoff? With her epilepsy, Amanda can keep her income from SSI if she stays out of the job market, and her SSI income may be as much as she can earn at a job. Amanda doesn't see herself as any kind of future professional person. That's beyond her imagination. People in her personal and family life have never been professionals. So she'll aim at the lower skill jobs—child care, nurse's aid, that sort of thing. These fields are crowded and they don't pay much. She might just do better to stay on SSI. I'm worried about her—will she continue to grow when Richard Jr. leaves Urban Day? Are there enough supports out there for her?"

Self-Help

Another way of fostering "maximum self-determination on the part of clients" is to encourage them to develop self-help skills. Urban Day staff encourages the development of a variety of self-help skills on the part of parents. One example is encouraging those who can to enroll in adult education programs, or to study for their GED. Another approach to self-help is teaching child-care skills to parents in the home. This occurred regularly when home training was funded at the agency, although this grant has now expired. Recently some of the teachers have agreed to provide parents with special classes at the agency to teach toilet training skills.

Parents are also kept informed about special programs for which they might qualify, from vocational training to public assistance. The social service staff instructs parents how to apply on their own whenever possible. A different way to develop self-help skills is to teach parents how to advocate for themselves, even within the agency. For this purpose Mrs. Haley has been trying to facilitate the development of a parents' group for years. This particular self-help project has proven discouraging at times, but students, volunteers, and staff have all been involved, and there is a parent leader. Parents are contacted by mail, telephone, and in person regarding meetings and meeting topics, and whenever possible transportation and babysitting are provided by the agency. Still, participation is often discouragingly low. With group participation so difficult to generate, the social service staff can't help but wonder if the effort is worthwhile at times. Perhaps parents don't feel a need to organize in their own behalf? Certainly the right of the parents *not* to participate must be respected. And yet, to drop completely the only vehicle for organized parent input into the agency seems premature. The social service staff continues to change its role as seems most promising. The division of labor that seems most fruitful at present involves a parent leader who organizes popular events like potluck suppers and a social service adviser who provides ideas on special topics and speakers for meetings.

CONFIDENTIALITY AND PRIVACY

The third principle relating to ethical responsibility to clients involves confidentiality and privacy. In the language of the code of ethics, "the social worker should respect the privacy of clients and hold in confidence all information obtained in the course of professional service." The first provision under this principle states: "The social worker should share with others confidences about clients, without their consent, only for compelling professional reasons." The second provision adds: "The social worker should inform clients fully about the limits of confidentiality in a given situation, the purposes for which information is obtained, and how it may be used."

Provisions one and two as just quoted reflect the fact that in practice, not all client information *can* be kept in confidence. Specifically, social workers do not have the legal right, as enjoyed by lawyers and the clergy, to keep information in confidence when subpoenaed by a court of law. Social workers need to know this and should inform their clients if they begin exploring information that might involve illegal acts.

Knowledge of legal limitations qualifying the principle of confidentiality is obviously important for social workers employed in probation and parole settings, but it can also be important at Urban Day. For example, if a social worker is discussing possible child abuse or neglect with the client, the client must be informed that what he or she says can be used in court. Sometimes Urban Day social workers do go to court to testify to the alleged abuse or neglect of a child, but only as a last resort and as the only perceived means to have a needy child placed in foster care. In these cases, it is ethically required and only fair to inform the parents clearly that whatever information they are helping supply can be used against them. In these cases, fortunately, the fear aroused in many parents regarding court litigation is enough to bring about positive behavior change as was demonstrated in the case of Amanda Jenkins.

How the principle of confidentiality relates the profession of social work to the external legal system is a major consideration. Social workers would prefer that the principle of confidentiality be recognized by law as a legal right of the profession, as it is for lawyers and the clergy. In most places, however, it is not recognized, at this point in time. This is a serious issue between the profession and society. The profession as a whole will need to have its right to licensure recognized on a state-by-state basis if confidentiality is to be built into the law. Under licensure, certain kinds of confidentiality between social workers and clients could be guaranteed. But states have been slow to permit licensure in an era of deregulation. In addition, society is reluctant to grant confidentiality since it wants the right to subpoena the most information possible. And to make the issue more complex, it probably would not be a good idea to make confidentiality an inviolable right of the profession under all circumstances. As an example, lawyers in most states are not required by law to report a client who has confided clear intent to murder a specific person. This is pobably an example of a situation in which the principle of confidentiality has been carried too far, although others would certainly argue differently. Social workers, by contrast, are required by law in many states to report all cases of suspected child abuse to the relevant authorities. Among the leaders of efforts to require this sort of reporting were social workers, in the interest of maximum protection for minor children.

At Urban Day, most of the issues involving confidentiality are far more day to day in nature than the issue as it relates to the court system and the law. Urban Day Center is a fairly small agency; most of the staff know most of the clients, and many of the clients know each other as well. The following case example may help illustrate some of the complications involved in maintaining confidentiality in a setting like this.

Jimmy Frances was referred to Urban Day by Blue County Protective Services. His case had originally been brought to the attention of Protective Services by a concerned neighbor. Jimmy had been born premature, had then developed pneumonia shortly after birth, and was a "failure to thrive" baby, so that he looked painfully emaciated. Protective services wanted to place Jimmy in a structured situation where he would receive daily supervised nutrition. Urban Day accepted the boy because his physical development was measurably delayed.

The Frances family was assigned to Carol Jean Heintz. This easygoing, parent-oriented community worker was uncharacteristically appalled when she first visited the Frances home—uncharacteristically because very little fazes Carol Jean. She found a nineteen-year-old mother there of Anglo-French descent. That wasn't so surprising. What was so surprising was that there were six little children in the home, including Jimmy, all under three years of age and all belonging to Betty Frances. The Frances's home was a dilapitated old wooden structure, and even for an experienced inner-city worker like Mrs. Heintz, its condition was appalling. It would be nice to be able to say that the condition of the house itself was terrible due to fault of the landlord, for example, that the ceiling was falling in or the plumbing left broken for six months. But in this case, the frame of the house was essentially intact, the plumbing worked, but the housekeeping was, as described by Carol Jean Heintz, a disaster. There were dirty clothes all over the floor in every room; garbage was rotting in piles on the kitchen floor extending out into the hallway; dirty diapers lay in heaps on beds and chairs and vied with the garbage in terms of setting the atmosphere. Cockroaches ran around freely. All the rooms were dark and dreary due to curtains being pulled together and pinned shut. The kitchen, however, appeared a bit brighter because all the burners on the stove were blazing fiercely and the oven, also set on high heat, was open. Ms. Frances's personal appearance was also depressing. Her clothes hung on her overweight body half open, pinned together haphazardly. The girl looked to be around forty, rather than her nineteen years.

As Carol Jean began to get to know Betty, she learned that the mother was not very well herself, physically. She had back problems and an interminable series of colds. She slept a lot, or at least whenever she could, given her six children. She seemed almost entirely lacking in energy, kind of dragging herself along through life. None of her children had been planned, although the same man had fathered all six. She liked the children but seemed a bit amazed at their number. The oldest, a little girl, had come along when Ms. Frances was sixteen. When the young mother was seventeen, a set of twins were born. A second set arrived when she was eighteen. Now, just this year, Jimmy had been born.

Betty Frances liked the father of her children but didn't want to marry him. She didn't seem to have many feelings for the man, though he did visit on occasion and brought the children toys. The one person in life Betty Frances seemed to harbor strong feelings for was her mother. Unfortunately, the mother had moved recently to another state. Betty missed her a lot and felt depressed.

Where does one begin? Carol Jean examined as carefully as she could all six children in their home setting. All were dressed in dirty, ill-fitting clothing, their hair unkempt. They looked malnourished and starved for attention as well. She imagined how much Urban Day could do for all of them, if they could qualify for service. She decided to have them all tested, not just Jimmy. In retrospect, she feels that this may have been a mistake. At any rate, the five youngest children were found to be delayed in speech development, probably due to lack of stimulation in the home. As openings occurred at the agency, they were enrolled one by one.

Then began the slow tortuous process of working with the family. In order to remain at Urban Day, the children had to have certain medical examinations and immunizations. The mother wouldn't take the children to medical appointments herself, so the staff had to do it for all five children. That got to be quite a burden. And since it was staff policy always to attempt to involve the parent in medical appointments, Ms. Frances was contacted frequently. Since there were five children to schedule, that annoyed her. Then, usually at least one child got sick at school every day and had to be sent home. A good part of that problem was the change in diet. At home the children ate nearly all starch. Urban Day's diet was much more nutritious but it took their digestive systems time to adapt. Meanwhile, diarrhea hit one child after the other and they went home sick. This too annoyed the mother.

Obviously, a famly like this was highly visible at Urban Day. With five children from the same family attending the center, everyone from classroom aides on up had some contact and interest. Moreover, once the children were bathed and dressed in clean clothes, they were attractive and appealing, so everyone wanted to protect them by making sure they got to school regularly. At least at Urban Day they would all be bathed and fed. When their attendance fluctuated unpredictably, everyone began asking questions of the social workers, especially Carol Jean Heintz, to find out why.

It would be appropriate for Mrs. Heintz to share information about the family with Mrs. Haley and other social service staff and with relevant professional staff such as teachers and the agency nurse for purposes of consultation and supervision. From the time of the initial contact, it is explained to parents that information pertinent to the care of a child is shared among professional staff. But in the case of the Frances family, nonprofessional persons such as volunteers and even other parents would ask the worker about the case. Why wouldn't Ms. Frances get her children immunized? What kind of woman was she? Why didn't she give her children a bath at home? And good heavens, why didn't she practice birth control? Or did she, but it didn't work for her? Was she trying anything more effective now? Exactly what?

According to professional ethics, Mrs. Heintz was bound not to answer these questions. Answering them would violate the principle of confidentiality. And yet, having to maintain confidence was difficult and stressful, because to do so could make Mrs. Heintz look incompetent. It might look as if she had neglected to deal with these issues, or as if she had tried to deal with them, but had failed to bring the mother around to the "correct" behavior. In fact, Carol Jean Heintz talked to the mother frequently about these very problems. But Betty Frances was making her own choices, a practice that is supported by the principle of self-determination.

On the issue of birth control, the one in which everyone seemed to be most interested, Betty Frances was simply unwilling to practice it. Her children were unplanned, but yet she loved them in her own way. She came from a family of ten children, so the large number of infants around was normal for her. The children provided her with her only reason for living and gave her some status among her peers and family. Moreover, although her standard of living was extremely low because of her dependence on public welfare, her monthly grant allowed her to feed and clothe her children somewhat. She intended to go on and have more. She said she had discussed having her tubes tied when her most recent child was born, but the hospital was Catholic and the doctor had refused. Now, she said, she was glad, as she was ready for some more babies again. As far as keeping medical appointments for the children was concerned, and arranging for immunizations, that seemed like a waste of time to the young mother. She wasn't used to going to a doctor herself and couldn't understand the reasons for taking the children. Moreover, Urban Day's constant demands, such as medical appointments, dietary changes, cleanliness, and schedules, wore her down. She wasn't sure the services the children got at the agency were worth the effort she was supposed to make to keep them there.

Carol Jean did as she had to do ethically. She did not discuss Betty Frances' beliefs regarding birth control and other issues with inappropriate people, even though at times her silence made her look bad. Carol Jean also did not discuss the chaos of the woman's home with inappropriate staff, or her personal lethargy or attitudes toward medical care, because that would betray confidences of the client. Exercising the principle of confidentiality in the case of the Frances family led to some awkward moments for Carol Jean Heintz, where she would have to answer persistent inquirers with something like, "I'm sorry, I can't answer that." If that response wasn't sufficient to deter the questioners, she would point out how confidentiality could protect everyone at times, and for that reason should be respected.

Eventually, Ms. Frances stopped sending her children to Urban Day. It was too much of a bother for her to keep up with all of Urban Day's requirements. Characteristically, Betty Frances did not inform Urban Day of her decision, she just stopped sending the children. When Carol Jean called her about attendance on the telephone, the mother said the bus hadn't stopped. Carol Jean then talked with the bus driver, to be sure he honked loudly enough for the mother to hear. When that didn't work,

Carol Jean tried morning wake-up calls. Then she rode out on the bus herself several mornings and knocked at the door. Eventually, the mother just wouldn't answer. As with the case of Michelle Champlin, the case had to be closed by Urban Day. There was nothing else the agency could do. A referral was made to a private agency that offered speech therapy in the home, financed by Medicaid. But the mother wouldn't open the door for the speech therapist, either. Protective services was informed, but they didn't intervene again because they felt that Urban Day's reports showed the children functioning near age level and not actively abused. It has recently been learned by Urban Day, however, that a later complaint by a neighbor to protective services eventually resulted in foster care for all the children.

As this case helps illustrate, confidentiality can be more difficult to maintain in practice than one might expect. A good many of the workers at Urban Day are paraprofessionals with a different value orientation than the social service staff. For example, the child-care workers and foster grandparents maintain a healthy interest in the development of the children, but they do not share the same professional constraints as the teachers and social workers, such as confidentiality as a professional ethic. Also, many parents spend time at Urban Day, and get acquainted that way. They want to know information about each other that, ethically speaking, should not be passed from professional social service staff to clients or certain other staff or volunteers. So Urban Day social service workers have to be careful to avoid answering direct questions as tactfully as possible. Sometimes this involves discussing with the inquirer the limits placed on the worker by the ethic of confidentiality.

Confidentiality can also become a problem in situations where more than one adult member of a family is working with the same social services staff person, but different family members tell the worker markedly different stories. This can get worse when the worker involved is asked by an informant not to discuss his to her information with the other members of the family, yet the informant clearly expects some remedial action to be taken as a result of the "hot tip." Mrs. Haley found herself in this kind of bind in the case of Timmy Fowler. Timmy was referred to Urban Day because of speech and gross motor delays. He also had an extremely short attention span and exhibited almost violent behavior. He was continuously on the move, all over everywhere and everybody, and would get into screaming fits if restrained. At the time of referral, Timmy was living with his maternal aunt and uncle, because his mother was hospitalized due to severe depression.

When Timmy's family came in for the intake interview, several adults came in with him, all anxious to be involved in the process. Timmy's twenty-year-old mother, Gina Fowler, came, on leave from the hospital. Her sister and brother-in-law, Alice and George White, who were currently caring for Timmy, also took part. Another maternal aunt and uncle,

John and Mary Herbert, were present as well. Then there was Gina's father, Henry Fowler. All were interested in the agency, the service that could be provided for the child, and the child himself. This was a very unusual showing of interest by such a large number of people, and of course an indication of family strength. All were potential resources for the child.

The problem was that each and every one of them called Mrs. Haley at different times to give her their input on what each thought was wrong with the others. They didn't want anyone to know they had called, however. Eventually the situation stabilized, and input came largely from Timmy's mother, Gina, and her sister and brother-in-law, Alice and George White. Gina would urgently inform Mrs. Haley that Alice and George did such and such that was not good for her son, but please don't tell them she said so. Then Alice and George would call Mrs. Haley regarding whatever poor decision they thought Gina had made for herself in the hospital now, but please don't tell her they said so. They were sure, however, that Gina's behavior indicated she was nowhere near ready for release and resumption of care for her son.

Mrs. Haley wished to honor confidentiality for everyone concerned and did her best to honor requests for privileged communication. And then it occurred to her she really didn't know any more what was OK to say to whom. She was overloaded with confidential data and restrictions on how she could use it. Finally, she knew the situation couldn't continue. Other people had to share the burden and responsibility of information and case planning, and face up to their feelings about one another in order to work them through. It was time to call the family members together.

She approached the people most directly concerned with the situation, Gina, Alice, and George, by telephone. "Look," she told them candidly. "I'm feeling very much in the middle. You say you want to tell me this and that and it's so important, but yet you tell me not to tell the person it's about. I feel now that if there is information I cannot act on, I should not even have it. So from now on we'll all meet together to work things out."

This was not what the family wanted. They protested openly at first, and then when Mrs. Haley stuck to her point of view, they resisted covertly by scheduling appointments and missing them due to last-minute conflicts. However, they were basically all responsible people and when Mrs. Haley continued to refuse to talk to any one of them individually, they finally got their schedules together and came in as a family group. Accompanying Gina was her therapist from the hospital.

Mrs. Haley assured each and every family member that no one was going to have to sacrifice his or her wants or beliefs in the joint meetings. They could all discuss each problem as long as necessary to reach agreement. She assured each person that no individual would have to give in on anything. Either the group would work on the problem until each person felt satisfied with the resolution, or any decision would be postponed until the next appointment, or as long as necessary.

Reassured by this kind of explicit working agreement, the family members got down to business and confronted each other with a few minor complaints and desires. These were resolved to everyone's satisfaction within the meeting. In later sessions, more serious issues were introduced and discussed. Now, the family is working constructively together. Gina is out of the hospital, living with her father but planning to move to a halfway house shortly. She will be able to have Timmy with her in that supportive, structured environment. Urban Day will be able to work with her and her son for several more months after her move, until Timmy is three, to maintain his gains in the context of a new living situation.

As for Timmy, his three-second attention span has increased to normal. Both expressive and receptive language skills are nearing age level. He seems like a totally different child, happily sitting in the laps of his teachers and family members for almost as long as they want him. When he leaves Urban Day at three, outpatient speech therapy will be all he'll require prior to regular kindergarten.

Further Considerations

Three more provisions under the principle regarding confidentiality and privacy should be addressed. These are as follows: "The social worker should afford clients reasonable access to any official social work records concerning them;" "when providing clients with access to records, the social worker should take due care to protect the confidences of others contained in those records;" and "the social worker should obtain informed consent of clients before taping, recording, or permitting third party observation of their activities."

These provisions are reasonably self-explanatory. At Urban Day, as at most other social service agencies, a file is kept preserving the paperwork done for each client. Case notes may also be entered into the file. In fact, each time a worker visits, telephones, or is telephoned by a client at Urban Day, a brief note is made of this fact, including the date, time, and basic content of the contact. Then, if a client's primary worker is absent from the agency at a time when the client calls in needing urgent attention, another social service worker can review the record of transactions with that client to help determine whatever actions might be necessary. In accordance with provisions one and two of this principle, clients are informed that other social service staff may review their records, and why. These records are for professional use only and off-limits to nonprofessional staff such as the child-care workers. Clients are specifically informed what types of staff do and do not have access to case files.

If clients wish to review their own case files, a fairly infrequent occurrence at Urban Day, they are permitted to do so. In this circumstance the funding realities discussed earlier which require family weaknesses to be emphasized can cause problems. People don't enjoy reading negative portrayals of themselves. So staff have to take care to be present to answer questions and explain, a very difficult task. The primary worker will also review the case file before giving it to the client in order to screen it for confidential information.

FEES

The last principle in this portion of the code of ethics concerning responsibility to clients relates to fees. The code states: "When setting fees, the social worker should ensure that they are fair, reasonable, considerate, and commensurate with the service performed and with due regard for the clients' ability to pay."

At Urban Day, as discussed previously, clients do not pay fees for any of the services provided. Most clients are too poor to pay for anything, and if required to do so, they simply forgo involvement with the agency. This fact was demonstrated fairly clearly when the agency tried at one time to charge a small fee for transportation, as discussed previously. Clients on public assistance were definitely deterred, and the policy was discontinued. However, the issue of fees is still alive at Urban Day as public moneys for special education are cut. As a result intact, nonabusing families are now being refused funding by the Combined Community Services Board. Some of these families would be able and willing to pay fees to have their children enrolled. Some kind of sliding scale could perhaps be devised to permit them to utilize the services at Urban Day. The problem would be that few could afford to pay full cost for the program. Thus if the Combined Community Services Board continues to refuse to provide any subsidies whatever for such families, sliding fees would not solve the problem. And at present, funding sources do not permit the agency to charge any fees for service.

There is one further provision under the principle of the code relating to fees: "The social worker should not divide a fee or accept or give anything of value for receiving or making a referral." This provision of the code aims to prevent the salaried agency practitioner from developing a profitable little business on the side by sending clients who have come to his or her more well-known, established agency to a professional in private practice who is trying to develop a paying clientele. Referral in social work practice should be appropriate to the needs of the client, not the practitioner, and should be carried out as part of the routine professional obligation of each social worker. Urban Day social workers make referrals constantly as part of their expected job description and charge no fees for this service.

To summarize, this chapter has been devoted to exploring and illustrating the second category of principles of the social work code of ethics, the social worker's ethical responsibility to clients. The principles included are primacy of client's interests, rights and prerogatives of clients, confidentiality and privacy, and fees. As has been shown by use of examples from Urban Day, some of these principles of the code of ethics are easier to apply in practice than others and some are more relevant for particular agencies than others, but all require careful attention by the social work practitioner.

REVIEW

Chapter 3 has illustrated the second section of the revised NASW code of ethics, the social worker's ethical responsibility to clients. The code emphasizes and underscores the primary importance of the social worker's professional obligation to clients through its detailed development of this category of principles, reproduced in full below.

THE SOCIAL WORKER'S ETHICAL RESPONSIBILITY TO CLIENTS

F. Primacy of Clients' Interests. The social worker's primary responsibility is to clients.
   1. The social worker should serve clients with devotion, loyalty, determination, and the maximum application of professional skills and competence.
   2. The social worker should not exploit relationships with clients for personal advantage, or solicit the clients of one's agency for private practice.
   3. The social worker should not practice, condone, facilitate or collaborate with any form of discrimination on the basis of race, color, sex, sexual orientation, age, religion, national origin, marital status, political belief, mental or physical handicap, or any other preference or personal characteristic, condition, or status.
   4. The social worker should avoid relationships or commitments that conflict with the interests of clients.
   5. The social worker should under no circumstances engage in sexual activities with clients.
   6   The social worker should provide clients with accurate and complete information regarding the extent and nature of the services available to them.
   7. The social worker should apprise clients of their risks, rights,

opportunities, and obligations associated with social service to them.

8. The social worker should seek advice and counsel of colleagues and supervisors whenever such consultation is in the best interest of the clients.

9. The social worker should terminate service to clients, and professional relationships with them, when such service and relationships are no longer required or no longer serve the clients' needs or interests.

10. The social worker should withdraw services precipitously only under unusual circumstances, giving careful consideration to all factors in the situation and taking care to minimize possible adverse effects.

11. The social worker who anticipates the termination or interruption of service to clients should notify clients promptly and seek the transfer, referral, or continuation of service in relation to the clients' needs and preferences.

G. Rights and Prerogatives of Clients. The social worker should make every effort to foster maximum self-determination on the part of clients.

1. When the social worker must act on behalf of a client who has been adjudged legally incompetent, the social worker should safeguard the interests and rights of that client.

2. When another individual has been legally authorized to act in behalf of a client, the social worker should deal with that person always with the client's best interest in mind.

3. The social worker should not engage in any action that violates or diminishes the civil or legal rights of clients.

H. Confidentiality and Privacy. The social worker should respect the privacy of clients and hold in confidence all information obtained in the course of professional service.

1. The social worker should share with others confidences revealed by clients, without their consent, only for compelling professional reasons.

2. The social worker should inform clients fully about the limits of confidentiality in a given situation, the purposes for which information is obtained, and how it may be used.

3. The social worker should afford clients reasonable access to any official social work records concerning them.

4. When providing clients with access to records, the social worker should take due care to protect the confidences of others contained in those records.

5. The social worker should obtain informed consent of clients before taping, recording, or permitting third party observation of their activities.

I.   Fees. When setting fees, the social worker should ensure that they are fair, reasonable, considerate, and commensurate with the service performed and with due regard for the clients' ability to pay.
    1.   The social worker should not divide a fee or accept or give anything of value for receiving or making a referral.

STUDY QUESTIONS

1   How does the case of Antonia serve to illustrate the principle, primacy of clients' interests?

2   What additional actions might have been taken by Mrs. Gantz when she first transferred the case of Antonia to the public schools, to help prevent the neglect of the little girl by the physical therapist?

3   How does the documentation required for obtaining funding for children to be placed at Urban Day sometimes create an ethical dilemma in itself for Urban Day social workers?

4   In the termination of the case of Michelle Champlin, what ethical principles did the social workers involved take care to recognize and practice?

5   What complications and complexities regarding the concept of self-determination does the Johnston case illustrate? Why didn't the social worker just terminate with this family? What does the author mean by stating that "Self-determination, for Ms. Johnston, was a product of the interaction among a number of systems other than (and including) her own person?"

6   How does the fourth provision under the primacy of clients' interests principle of the code apply to the case of the Jenkins family? What creative methods of problem solving are employed to work with this case?

7   How does licensure of social work as a profession help ensure the principle of confidentiality and privacy?

8   How does the case of the Frances family illustrate some of the complexities and personal frustrations involved in maintaining confidentiality for a client?

9   What complications does the Urban Day staff face in providing clients access to their records? Would other agencies face similar problems? Why do you think the code includes the provision that social workers should provide clients with reasonable access to their own records?

4

The Social Worker's Ethical Responsibility to Colleagues

"Good morning, everyone. Bus number three reports it's turning the corner from Biltmore Avenue onto Clive Street now, and it should be here in about five minutes. Please get ready to bring the children in."

"Well, folks, bus number three is here. Now is the time for all good people to come to the aid of their countrymen—oops, and women. Please hustle if you can."

Then, several minutes later, "Thanks, everybody. Now another alert: Bus number one is on Washington Avenue and should be here in just a few minutes. All staff who can carry please be out front."

Again, a few moments later, "Thanks, everybody. We're OK with bus number one. Now for those who can bring children in from bus number two, it should be arriving in about five minutes."

Such is the sound and action at Urban Day around eight o'clock every weekday morning. Meeting the buses and bringing the children into the center, some able to wobble along on their own two feet but most needing to be carried, is a task that involves every staff person at Urban Day one time or another. Even the top administrators turn out to help when needed, as when several buses happen to arrive at the same time. Generally, this is a job people enjoy, even if other pressing work has to be put aside for the moment. The children arrive buckled into special seats and have to be released and lifted off the bus with care, then escorted or carried into the center. Usually they arrive responsive and smiling, clearly happy to be there. Working with them in this way helps get the day off to a pleasant start.

But another factor at Urban Day besides the children helps the day begin on a positive note, and that is the working atmosphere of the center as a whole. The staff is trusted to know what needs to be done and to work

80

together as much as possible. Announcements about bus arrivals, for example, are made as messages conveying information, not as orders. The secretary-receptionist who usually coordinates the front desk activities and makes most of the announcements keeps up a constant humorous banter which lets people know what is needed, mobilizes them to assist where required, and thanks them for their efforts. A sense of personal responsiveness and contribution from each staff member is maintained as child-care workers, teachers, social service staff, volunteers, and anybody else with a few flexible moments pitches in to help transport the children to their classrooms. During the rest of the day the banter on the public address system may continue, spicing and garnishing necessary announcements. Over the system it is not unknown for a pithy poem or limerick to be read in humorous spirit, all of which helps to create a warm and very human working environment.

This chapter will discuss the third heading of the social work code of ethics, the social worker's ethical responsibility to colleagues. This section of the code outlines how the worker should behave toward coworkers and associates. The code does not specify clearly whether its use of the word colleague is intended to apply to fellow social workers only or to other members of one's agency staff. Provision eight under the first principle of this section, respect, fairness, and courtesy, does state that "the social worker should extend to colleagues of other professions the same respect and cooperation that is extended to social work colleagues." This helps assure the reader that the various principles and provisions of this portion of the code are intended to apply to all other *professional* staff as well as to the professional social work staff. However, agencies like Urban Day provide their social workers with many staff associates who are not traditionally considered professional, such as receptionists, case aides, and child-care workers. At Urban Day, as at many other agencies, these members of the staff provide crucial services, and the social service director works closely with them. Even the bulk of the social service staff itself is "nonprofessional" at Urban Day, in the very real sense that the community workers do not have accredited social work academic training or degrees and cannot, therefore, belong to the National Association of Social Workers.

Ideally, however, the standard of behavior described in the code of ethics is one that the fully qualified professional director of the social service department, Mrs. Haley, should demonstrate with respect to her staff and other coworkers. Hence our interpretation of the word colleague will be broad and extended to include all relevant coworkers at the agency. It should be noted, however, that the members of other professions and the paraprofessional workers would not themselves be professionally bound by the principles of the social work code of ethics. But Mrs. Haley, as head of the social service staff at Urban Day, can and has developed a clear departmental expectation that her community workers will understand and abide by the provisions of the code. She has spent a good deal of time exploring with her workers the ethical ramifications of various practice decisions, in this way helping them relate ethical ideals to the real world of practice.

RESPECT, FAIRNESS, AND COURTESY

The first principle of this section of the code states the following: "Respect, Fairness, Courtesy—The social worker should treat colleagues with respect, courtesy, fairness, and good faith."

At Urban Day, as described earlier, the various members of the staff, and not just the social service workers, go out of their way to create a tolerant, human atmosphere for the agency as a whole, maximizing the potential for all workers to treat each other with respect and good faith. From the continuous banter of the lively secretary-receptionist on the public address system to the prompt and reliable response of the staff, there is a consistent effort by all staff members to help meet each other's needs. Of course, things do not always go smoothly. It would be inaccurate and foolish to describe the daily operations at Urban Day as consistently warm and rewarding. There are days when staff absences due to illness, vacations, or personal days leave the agency shorthanded. At such times everyone's energy diffuses and dissipates, creating short tempers and impatient outbursts. There are also unsettling disagreements at times with regard to agency decisions and procedures. But in general, all the staff people from administrator to aide can be relied upon to extend their best efforts. Normally, an atmosphere of respect and good faith prevails at the agency as a whole. That helps the social work staff perform the high quality work that it does.

Cooperating with Colleagues

The first of eleven provisions under the principle of respect, fairness, and courtesy reads: "The social worker should cooperate with colleagues to promote professional interests and concerns." There are many, many ways in which Urban Day social service staff cooperates with colleagues. For example, when children come to the center for evaluations, it is the social service staff who contact all the other relevant professionals to schedule appointments. Then, after a child has been accepted for service, a detailed planning session for the child's treatment must be held. It is the social workers who schedule the meeting and then make sure later that everyone understands the details of the treatment plan. Case coordinating, planning, and evaluating requires conscious cooperation to promote professional and client concerns. Other ways the social service staff cooperates is to work together physically when clients live in particularly rough areas of the city, where walking alone could be dangerous. Thus, cooperation stretches from concrete physical help to more abstract activities such as case planning.

Another very interesting role for the social workers at Urban Day in promoting staff cooperation is helping to solve disputes. Consider the following incident which appreciably darkened the atmosphere at the agency for a period of time:

"Tra la la, tra la la, fa la la la," sang Mrs. Sally Brown happily. She was busy taping colorful children's pictures to the shiny new walls of her classroom. Sally was the teacher for one of the classrooms for toddlers, but for more than a week now her room had been out of commission, filled with paint chips and old newspaper. It had been completely cleaned, scraped, and repainted, and now looked very fine indeed. The badly needed renovations and redecoration had been made possible through recent grant moneys secured from a private donor. Sally Brown had gladly endured the inconvenience of having to work all day with her fifteen children in the unstructured common play area for a week or more in order to have a shiny bright classroom to work in at the end of it all. Sally was a creative teacher, proud of her work. She encouraged the children who could to express themselves through art. From her professional training she knew the children would feel more comfortable with the classroom changes if their own pictures were on the wall, and they would feel proud to see their own work on display as well.

Sally stood back to admire her work. Ah, lovely. Against the freshly painted walls of the gleaming classroom the children's pictures looked bright and cheerful. Sally had taken time to put complementary colors together, and the result was quite satisfying. She pictured the smiles on the children's faces tomorrow as they arrived to view their precious art works on display for all to see. Sally sang a few notes more in sheer contentment. "Tra la la, tra la la, tra la." But she was working late, after normal work hours when the children were gone, to get things done with a minimum of disturbance to the classroom. She was tired, and so after a few moments she turned to gather her things and go home.

Sally turned around quite unsuspectingly to meet the tense and disapproving stare of an upper-level agency administrator, Trish Ramleau. Mrs. Ramleau, the program director, held a position above that of Sally's own immediate supervisor. Sally knew immediately from the expression on her superior's face that she was doing something about which this high-level agency administrator was most unhappy. But before Sally had time to gather her senses, Mrs. Ramleau spoke. "Whatever do you think you're doing to that wall?" she demanded abruptly. "For goodness' sake, take those pictures down at once. They are going to ruin all that new paint, which has cost this agency a fortune." Trish Ramleau had now delivered her edict, and she felt uncomfortable just standing there, as she knew her words wouldn't be popular. So she hesitated a moment more and then turned to walk quickly away. Sally was left with her own face taut and upset and her head a profusion of unspoken retorts.

After her alarm subsided, Sally found herself furious. "What is this place supposed to be for?" she fumed. "Helping the children develop to their fullest or keeping the place immaculate for bigwigs?" She tore the pictures down from the wall in frustration and stomped out of the agency, wishing she didn't have to come to work again the next morning. There was no way she could override Trish Ramleau's orders, she knew, because even her own supervisor, the education director, didn't have as much administrative power at the agency. When Sally got back to work the next morning, she told her sad tale to her colleagues and soon everyone on the teaching staff was angry with Trish Ramleau as well. They had been planning to decorate the new walls of their own classrooms with children's pictures. The shiny new classroom walls suddenly looked bare and uninviting, and in the tense atmosphere all the toddlers became unbearably cantankerous. The situation seemed hopeless because everybody knew administrators were more interested in money than in the welfare of children. People were going to have to live in a dull, miserable school from now on. The classroom became bleaker by the minute. Nobody was enjoying the pretty colors of the bright new paint, not now. Those teachers who were scheduled to have their classrooms redecorated next began to grumble that they'd rather live with the old scratched and faded walls than go through the renovation process. At least they could cover the old walls with pictures; they always had.

The story reached Mrs. Haley almost immediately, because her contact with teachers is regular and routine. Almost every day she carries some of the children in from the buses, and then she stops and chats with the teachers to find out if they have noticed any particular problems that they want social service to check out. So Mrs. Haley got an earful the very morning after the unfortunate incident. As was probably true of everyone who heard the story, Mrs. Haley's immediate response was indignation. Here Sally Brown had been working on her own time to make her classroom more comfortable for the children, and she had been reprimanded for it. Moreover, artwork on walls is known to be stimulating and helpful for child development. Pictures encourage children to focus their eyes, to concentrate, and perhaps to try some artwork of their own. That in turn encourages eye–hand coordination and a more positive self-image.

But Mrs. Haley also cautioned herself that Trish Ramleau must have had strong reasons to act as she did. So she limited her response to Mrs. Brown's story to expressing compassion for the difficult experience she had had, and to obtain permission to discuss the situation with Mrs. Ramleau. Then she went to talk with Trish Ramleau herself. Because Urban Day is a small agency it is usually possible to talk with an administrator merely by knocking at the door and asking. Mrs. Haley found her administrative superior to be quite upset herself. Mrs. Ramleau had worked for months grooming the donor of the money for the special grant to redecorate the classrooms. Those old battered rooms were not proper places for the children. But now the teachers were wanting to put pictures up on those lovely sparkling walls. Why, the tape they used would pull off all the new paint! Did the teachers think Trish was going to be able to get another grant soon? Why, there just weren't many potenital private donors, and the grooming process took months or even years. And it wasn't easy. Didn't the teachers appreciate all the time and energy she had put into finding and securing those funds?

Mrs. Haley recognized that here was a situation that badly needed reframing. She saw the social work role as that of helping each side see the point of view of the other. Initially, both teachers and administrator felt unappreciated and undervalued, and viewed the other side as unreasonable. The teachers thought that what they did at the agency was the most important; after all, the very reason for the place was for the development of the children and they knew most about how to do it. But, in their opinion, Trish clearly didn't understand that. Conversely, Trish Ramleau felt that the place couldn't go on without her work, since she secured a good percentage of the funding for Urban Day. But, in her opinion, the teachers clearly didn't understand that.

Mrs. Haley used her interpersonal skills to help the teachers and Mrs. Ramleau realize that they shared the same major goals. Mrs. Ramleau wanted a bright, cheerful place for the children just as the teachers did. That is why she secured the funds for redecoration. Her fear now was only that pictures would ruin the new paint. Mrs. Haley reframed the dispute for her colleagues: It wasn't a matter of people valuing one contribution and not another, she suggested, or of one side being right and the other wrong. Both sides really wanted the same thing, an attractive, suitable classroom for the children. The real issue at hand could perhaps be restated, something like "pictures on the wall." Could pictures on the wall enhance the brightness and beauty of the classroom? If so, could they be hung on the walls without harming the new paint?

With the issue thus reframed, it didn't take long for Mrs. Ramleau to decide that pictures might indeed look nice in the classroom. She and Mrs. Haley together generated the idea that this could be done safely via requisitioning huge bulletin boards to be hung on classroom walls. Mrs. Ramleau thought she could obtain the necessary funds. The teachers agreed this would be a fine solution and agency harmony was restored.

Colleague Confidences

Keeping client information in strict confidence is probably one of the better known ethical responsibilities of the social worker. Confidentiality of client transactions and some of the difficulties involved have been discussed in detail in this book in Chapter 3. Less known and probably equally important is the ethical requirement to keep the professional confidences of colleagues. The relevant provision of the code of ethics states: "The social worker should respect confidences shared by colleagues in the course of their professional relationships and transactions."

This provision can obviously apply to formally shared professional confidences where, for example, social workers and their colleagues come together to discuss problematic cases and develop plans of action. The plans developed through joint conference may be quite different from anyone's initial suggestions. It would be unethical for a social worker to leave a conference and publicly broadcast, for example, how so-and-so's ideas initially differed radically from those of the rest of the group. What goes on inside a professional meeting should be kept in strict confidence, except, of course, for any formally written intervention plans which may arise out of such a meeting.

There is a less formal sense, however, in which confidentiality should be maintained among colleagues with respect to professional relationships. Every agency or work setting will place pressures on its workers, who may in response need to let off steam at times. In the course of ventilating frustrations a staff worker may say things about the agency or certain coworkers that are best forgotten (unless, of course, serious issues are raised which clearly must be dealt with). As an example, the social service staff at Urban Day felt under unusual pressure several years ago when funding levels fell, leading to serious considerations of a cut in staff. That probably would mean social service, as teachers and child-care workers were protected by a law that required a certain ratio of children to teachers and certified aides. No such law protected social workers. Everyone knew this. All the community workers valued their jobs. No one knew who might be let go, and nobody wanted to be that person.

As uncertainty rose, Mrs. Haley began to find that her community workers came to her more often to complain about the mistakes of somebody else on the social service staff. It all was done in the name of providing better client service, of course. But as job security decreased, the frequency of "blowing one's own horn," as Mrs. Haley described it, and putting down others increased. The hidden agenda seemed to be: If somebody has to go, let it be her, not me. Actually, any and all complaints held some merit; nobody is perfect. In some cases Mrs. Haley did follow up on the proffered information to make sure problematic cases were being handled as well as possible. But in most circumstances, she just listened, said some appropriate, compassionate words to the person reporting the problems, and let the complaints fade away gently so that no one would be hurt. She also took pains to ask the complainant questions such as, "Do you think you can help her? What do you think we can do so that so-and-so doesn't do that any more?" This encouraged work-related consultation among the staff. From Mrs. Haley's point of view, the tactic wasn't a gimmick. "If you seriously believe in people growing," she said, "you do what you can to stretch their perceptions and skills. Maybe this department doesn't have the perfect person doing each job, but how many people would you have to go through to find that? My job is to see that the staff develops."

Mrs. Haley's point of view is that *all* of the important ethical practices social workers are urged to apply to their clients should be applied to transactions with colleagues as well. If a worker really is not doing well, start where that worker is and develop from there. Explore all possible options. People are not consumer items to be expended, but resources to be developed. Fortunately, most of the scapegoating in the name of professional expertise began to wane with Mrs. Haley's thoughtful handling. Moreover, the agency director skillfully endeavored to reduce staff fears by insisting any necessary staff cuts would be accomplished by attrition alone. Shortly thereafter, scapegoating stopped completely.

Facilitating Competent Performance

"The social worker should create and maintain conditions of practice that facilitate ethical and competent professional performance by colleagues," states the next provision of the code. One way Mrs. Haley strives to meet this requirement is to discuss problematic cases with her workers using the code as an explicit guideline for making decisions. She is careful that her workers know and understand the ethical ramifications of various practice decisions. Cases are discussed from an ethical frame of reference with the assigned workers and often as a department as well.

Another way Mrs. Haley works to facilitate competent performance is by arranging in-service training sessions, sometimes for her staff but often for workers throughout the agency. For example, she has arranged in-service workshops on treatment of burn victims, on racism, on battered women, on working with hard-to-reach parents, on issues in developing parents' groups, and on many, many more interdisciplinary topics as the need has arisen. Mrs. Haley also consults with individuals and groups including her own staff, the teachers, and others as requested or needed, in order to improve services at Urban Day. She regards social work as a progressive learning process for everyone concerned and continues to upgrade her skills as well as help others develop theirs. Currently, Mrs. Haley is learning sign language in order to work better with a deaf child at the center, and characteristically, some of the other staff at the agency have been inspired to do so as well.

Because Mrs. Haley refuses to view any member of the staff as expendable, she feels that just as one needs to assess clients' readiness to take on new learning, so it is necessary to do the same thing for staff. She notes that her colleagues have different levels of skill in various areas. Where these skills are deficient, the answer is not to dismiss that staff member, but to help him or her build up skills to the required level. The nonjudgmental attitude required for working with clients must be extended to staff, and basic respect for the dignity and self-determination of each staff member must be observed. If a staff person seems to be falling short of the requirements of the job, then one should work with that staff person to assess his or her skills and develop a plan for remedial action. If the problem lies in the individual's current job description and if remedial action does not seem feasible, then explore all possible options for reassignment. As an example, let us examine Mrs. Haley's intervention strategies in the problematic situation of an elderly staff worker, a foster grandparent, whom we will call Papa Martinez.

Urban Day was delighted when the local foster grandparent program referred Papa Martinez to the center, because men are rarely willing to work with very young, handicapped children. When Mrs. Haley, who is the supervisor of the foster grandparent program at Urban Day, first met him she was even more delighted. Papa Martinez's energy seemed boundless and he looked forward to working with the children, particularly on the playground. Chronologically Papa's age fell somewhere in the late sixties, but in appearance he looked much younger. Tall, slim, with a chiseled face, plenty of gray-black hair and a light in his eye, Papa Martinez promised to offer the children a great deal. He was undaunted by the severity of many of the children's handicaps and was the sort of person who would challenge them to accomplish new feats.

And therein lay the problem. To Papa Martinez, children were children were children. That meant he would treat handicapped children like other youngsters. That was wonderful in a way, because he did not look at the handicapped youngsters as different or peculiar, as so many people obviously did. But Papa Martinez had a way of playing with them all in just the way he enjoyed his lively, healthy grandchildren. With great gusto he would toss the handicapped children into the air and bounce them up and down. They would scream with delight and excitement. The children with loose muscle tone and floppy bodies and flat affect (low expression of emotion) greatly benefited. They enjoyed every moment. However, Papa also picked up and bounced vigorously into the air all the little cerebral palsy victims with taut bodies, the little burn victims, the hydrocephalic children with their shunts, the hyperkinetics. Some of these children tightened and contracted so much in response that they could hardly move. Something would have to be done.

The obvious thing, of course, was to talk with Papa Martinez. Mrs. Haley did so as soon as she realized what was happening. So did the teachers and the child-care workers. But now another interesting phenomenon manifested itself: cultural biases. Papa Martinez was an elderly

Spanish gentleman. He was not used to listening to young females and taking their suggestions seriously. This is not uncommon among older men in general, but in the Spanish culture the characteristic is perhaps exaggerated. He refused to follow any suggestions put to him by Mrs. Haley or the teachers, all relatively young females. He continued to toss the children into the air and to engage in other creative forms of exciting, rough play. Clearly, something else had to be done.

In some settings, Papa Martinez's behavior would have been considered cause for termination. But, Mrs. Haley could clearly understand the motivation for Papa Martinez's behavior: his experience with his own children and grandchildren and his cultural learning regarding the importance of information from young females. She could admit to feeling angry and frustrated regarding the sexism issues of the problem, but was then able to move beyond. She reminded herself that the same nonjudgmental approach should be applied to staff as well as to clients. What options were open besides firing? Papa Martinez was a willing, healthy, and energetic worker, and many children loved him. Were there other roles at the agency he could fit? Papa Martinez got along well with the cook, so Mrs. Haley considered trying him out as an assistant. The cook was willing. But on further consideration Mrs. Haley realized that option wouldn't be appropriate. Foster grandparents were not supposed to do work normally performed by paid staff; that could lead to layoffs and cause other undesirable side effects.

She thought further—who *would* Papa Martinez listen to? She recalled that in the Spanish culture, age brought respect. There was no one at the agency as old as he was except some of the other foster grandparents. Mrs. Haley took time to observe with whom he talked, and then chose a woman older than Papa with whom he obviously had rapport (there were no other male foster grandparents). She enlisted this woman's help in talking with the man. After several firm interventions by the perceptive older woman, the tactic worked. It brought a sufficiently significant change in Papa's performance that the children's health and safety were no longer endangered. Everyone could relax again.

Mrs. Haley, however, thought she observed a decrease in his enjoyment of the children, and so she continued to think about him. As she puts it, it may occasionally be appropriate to counsel someone out of a job, even if almost never to fire. So she gathered information from the local foster grandparent program regarding other settings in which Papa Martinez might be able to play with children as exuberantly as he desired. Eventually an opening in a day-care center for normal children came to her attention. She let Papa Martinez know about it, and he decided to visit the place. Finding the setting there more compatible with his natural talents, he interviewed for the job and was hired. Papa moved on with good feeling all around, and returned to Urban Day for visits for a long time afterward.

Representing Fairly and Expressing Judgment Appropriately on the Qualifications, Views, and Findings of Colleagues

Mrs. Ramleau walked into Mrs. Haley's office one morning and announced: "Well, we've chosen the new education director. It's going to be Bonnie Nichols. I just wanted you to know so you can begin to work with her in that capacity right away."

"Hey, wait a minute, Trish!" Mrs. Haley exclaimed. "Do you mean you selected the new director for education without talking with any of the other heads of department about it first? I think I know Bonnie's work, and while she's done well as the volunteer director, I don't expect she'll be able to do so well supervising the teachers. I know she has a teaching degree but she hasn't taught in a long time. She has never taught preschool. I think the teachers will be upset to have a director appointed who hasn't been active in the profession for years. Have you thought about that? Is this decision final? Has anyone else been in on it?"

This was a long discourse from Mrs. Haley, but as she is a woman who speaks her mind, Mrs. Ramleau wasn't surprised at her openness. However, she was indeed upset at the intensity of Mrs. Haley's objections to the new staff choice. Trish Ramleau became tense and not a little angry in response. She couldn't help feeling insulted that her choice should be criticized.

"Listen, Lauren," she replied. "Bonnie has worked here for over a year as the volunteer director and she has done a good job. Both Theodore (Director of Urban Day) and I have agreed that she is the best choice among the candidates, and that is final. I'll be announcing the decision to the other department directors this morning." And with that, Trish Ramleau left.

Throughout the rest of the day, one after the other, the teachers, the medical director, therapy director, and even some of the child-care workers came into Mrs. Haley's office to talk to her about the new appointment. They talked among each other, too, and the consensus was that the choice was a poor one. People knew and liked Bonnie Nichols personally, felt she had done a good job as volunteer director, but there were complaints. Bonnie did not have the appropriate educational degree. She was certified to teach at the primary school level but not at the preschool level. For this reason, of course, she had also not had preschool teaching experience. It did not seem right to the teachers that they be supervised by a person who was not fully qualified to teach what they were teaching. Staff also felt that they should have been consulted about the decision in advance, to express their views confidentially before the choice was announced as final. Now they were either going to have to accept what they viewed as a bad decision, or stick their necks out to an uncomfortable degree, perhaps ruining their working relationships with both Bonnie Nichols and Trish Ramleau in the process.

It may be comforting to those who must struggle daily with large bureaucracies to know that even in a small and very human agency, bureaucratic events occur that make people feel disregarded and wipe out the atmosphere of tolerance and good humor. This incident brought about a good deal of agonizing on the part of the staff, who finally decided that they must protest the decision. Mrs. Haley took it upon herself to express the protest through the appropriate channels, that is, the agency administration. The first level of administration above that of the department directors was that of program director, the position held by Trish Ramleau. So Mrs. Haley went to Mrs. Ramleau first. When she did not obtain satisfaction, she went to the agency director, Theodore Tell. This action was in accord with the relevant guideline provided by the code of ethics, provision four under the first principle in the section relating to colleagues: "The social worker should treat with respect, and represent accurately and fairly, the qualifications, views, and findings of colleagues and use appropriate channels to express judgments on these matters."

Mrs. Haley's intervention was perceived by her immediate superior, Mrs. Ramleau, as insubordination. There is nothing in the code of ethics which protects the social worker from adverse reaction when behavior that follows agency procedures and ethical guidelines is perceived as threatening. Mrs. Ramleau told Mrs. Haley clearly that she viewed her position on the hiring of Bonnie Nichols to be personally disloyal. As unrest escalated, she also told the social service director that she would "write her up" if she did not publicly change her position to support Bonnie's hiring. To write someone up means to put written notice of censure in one's personnel file. This sort of thing is done explicitly to justify a firing. In other words, Mrs. Haley's job was being threatened unless she changed her attitude, a frequent event in a bureaucracy when a subordinate challenges a superior.

At this point Mrs. Haley took time to consciously sort the issues and her values. As she considered the issue that her boss perceived as loyalty, she recognized that she, Mrs. Haley, truly was loyal, both to her profession and to the purpose of the agency. She was opposing Trish's choice of staff only because she believed that choice would not meet the needs of the agency. Trish Ramleau, Mrs. Haley concluded, was wrong to see the issue as one of personal loyalty. The issue was whether Bonnie Nichols was a wise choice for the job position of educational director.

Having clarified the real issue in her own mind, Mrs. Haley then considered in further detail the hiring of Bonnie Nichols as education director. Would Bonnie in the position of education director be likely to do such a terrible job that keeping her out of that post would be worth losing her own job? No, Mrs. Haley decided. Bonnie Nichols was not the best staffing choice for the job, in her opinion, but she would probably perform adequately. Then should Mrs. Haley succumb, as Mrs. Ramleau required, and publicly support Bonnie's hiring? This would certainly save her job as social service director. Mrs. Haley and Mrs. Ramleau had worked together for a long time. They had fought certain serious battles together in the past on the same side and basically liked each other. Mrs. Haley believed that Mrs. Ramleau would probably welcome the opportunity to end the dispute if she could do so on her own terms.

But then Mrs. Haley realized that she could not change her public stance. That would require her to take a position she did not believe in. She would have to lie to the staff, negate her perceptions, and place personal loyalty above her professional assessments. That would cost her her self-respect. No. The issue of the hiring of Bonnie Nichols was not worth the loss of her job, but she, Lauren Haley, was. If the result was dismissal, so be it.

So Mrs. Haley refused to offer public support for the hiring of the new education director. A staff meeting with all the departmental heads, the program director, Trish Ramleau, and the agency director, Theodore Tell, was held in which the top administrators together formally heard the views of the staff. Mrs. Haley remained the major staff spokesperson. Toward the end of the meeting, Mr. Tell regretfully acknowledged that most of his department directors opposed the hiring of Bonnie Nichols. "Nevertheless," he said, "Bonnie has already been hired and the question is, can you work with her." Then he offered the staff support they badly needed by now. "I want you all to know that despite our occasional disagreements such as this one, I would want exactly the same people in the positions you now hold if I were to choose all over again."

Mr. Tell's words tactfully promised that there weren't going to be any firings. They also placed Bonnie in her new position with finality. This was an administrative decision, and the administrators had the right to make it. Now the staff would have to find out if they could live with it. What followed is again a tribute to the basic openness and goodwill of the Urban Day staff and the agency as a whole. The staff decided that since they could not prevent Bonnie's hiring, they would do all they could to assist her. That would benefit all of them. Mrs. Haley's consciously chosen posture at the agency became: "How can we best go about working with Bonnie now that she's here?" So while openly confronting Ms. Nichols with their initial misgivings, the rest of the staff offered her all the information and assistance they could. It was difficult slogging at first for everyone, and the challenge continues as this chapter is written. It is hopefully unlikely, however, that the agency will hire a director again without at least consulting the other relevant staff members beforehand.

Expressing judgment appropriately can apply to many circumstances besides those involving the qualifications of prospective coworkers. Social workers are continually producing intervention plans, case reports, needs assessment studies, and the like. Workers in Mrs. Haley's department are continually having to make difficult decisions regarding intervention strategies with hard-to-reach clients. These are examples of other common types of circumstances to which this provision may apply. Mrs. Haley as supervisor may need to represent and support the views and findings of her workers to higher-level administrators if their efforts are questioned. This, of course, necessitates her keeping in close contact with her staff so that she has input into major decisions and is satisfied they are sound.

Exploiting Disputes

The case of Bonnie Nichols' hiring illustrates the potential importance of another provision of the code under the respect, fairness, and courtesy heading. Provision six states: "The social worker should not exploit a dispute between a colleague and employers to obtain a position or otherwise advance the social worker's interest." It is conceivable that during the time Mrs. Haley was particularly unpopular with her immediate supervisor, one of the other members of the social work staff in her department might have sought her position. Fortunately, no such thing occurred, but this is the kind of circumstance for which this particular guideline in the code has been written.

Arbitration and Mediation

There will come a time in the careers of most social workers when professional disputes will require arbitration and mediation. In a way, the director of Urban Day acted as arbitrator in the dispute over the hiring of Bonnie Nichols. He made the final decision that Bonnie would indeed be hired, but he also made it clear that nobody would be fired for speaking out against her appointment. Taken together, these two decisions allowed business to return to normal at Urban Day. In more extreme circumstances, disputes may require the attention of higher-level source of arbitration and mediation. For example, had Mrs. Haley actually been fired, she probably would have taken her case to the agency Board of Directors. Failing satisfaction there, she could conceivably have requested a review of her case by the NASW.

But sometimes professional disputes must be settled in court. At the time of the writing of this chapter, Mrs. Haley is considering going to court over the professional handling of a case by one of her colleagues in the broader sense, a social worker for the Blue County Department of Public Welfare. Strictly speaking, courts arbitrate more than they mediate. Judges have the power to make decisions for the participants and they may decide entirely in favor of one side or another of a dispute. The concept of mediation involves a greater need for compromise. The mediator must consult with all parties in a dispute and then attempt to construct a solution with which all can eventually agree. This necessitates a process of give and take.

The case referred to involves a young mother who was convicted of child abuse and neglect over a year ago, and whose child was forthwith removed to a foster home. Diana Kinsman, the young mother, was catapulted toward change by the court decision, and her primary goal in life became to secure the return of her child. Diana's emotional goal was probably not unusual for a mother in such a circumstance, but her very real and constructive efforts to achieve her goal were definitely unusual and quite impressive to Mrs. Haley. First of all, Ms. Kinsman herself called Urban Day to refer her daughter, Dorothy. Diana was worried that Dorothy was developmentally delayed and asked for an evaluation. The evaluation was arranged through the protective services worker and the foster mother, and the results demonstrated mild delays in fine motor skills and speech. The child was duly enrolled at Urban Day. Thus Diana became a client of Mrs. Haley. The young mother came into the center every day to observe and work with little Dorothy. Diana explained that her major goal in life was to have her child come home again. She asked for instruction in parenting skills and any other tutelage available to learn to assist with the development of her daughter.

During the early period of her contact with Urban Day, Diana was called back into court for a review of her case. Mrs. Haley went with her at this time to testify about Urban Day's observations, if requested. She describes her court experience as somewhere between astounding and horrifying. The attorney for Diana and the guardian *ad litum* (court-appointed attorney to represent the needs of the child) simply yelled at each other across the courtroom floor "like little children." Each was clearly caught up in a win–lose contest regarding the case, and mother and child got lost in the middle. Diana's attorney wanted to win for Diana in this case because he totally believed in her abilities as a parent. The guardian *ad litum* and the attorney for Blue County Protective Services wanted the child to remain in foster care regardless of the mother's current circumstances or condition as a parent. But no one in court offered objective information relevant to making a decision regarding who should have custody of the child, Diana or Blue County. For example, nobody, including the Blue County protective services social worker, offered any objective assessment of Diana's parenting skills. Nobody was interested in finding out what was happening at Urban Day with the child or with the mother. The court ordered continued placement in foster care for little Dorothy. To Mrs. Haley, the experience was something like a free-for-all where the court order was made according to who produced the most noise. Since two of the three attorneys favored foster care, together they talked loudest and won the round. Mrs. Haley was appalled.

Where does one go after such an unsettling experience? Mrs. Haley chose to follow the guideline from the code of ethics which has been stated earlier, provision eight under respect, fairness, and courtesy: "The social worker should extend to colleagues of other professions the same respect and cooperation that is extended to social work colleagues." And in this circumstance she also acted on her belief described earlier that colleagues, social work or otherwise, deserve the same respect, consideration, and ethical treatment as clients. Therefore she tried to understand things from their point of view. Mrs. Haley then could recognize, upon careful reflection, that the attorneys and the Blue County social worker in this case were all enmeshed in the adversarial system required by the court. Each was operating from a win–lose frame of reference, and what was important to each at this point was winning the case, not what plan of care was best for the child named Dorothy Kinsman.

Mrs. Haley decided she would work with the attorneys and the protective services social worker with the same attention to the code of ethics as she would with a client. She would treat them all with consideration and respect yet at the same time do her best to broaden their perspectives so that they let go of the win–lose mentality. She arranged a problem-solving meeting in which all parties to decision making in the case could come together in a nonthreatening atmosphere. She invited all parties concerned to meet at Urban Day, a neutral setting, and went out of her way to reserve the agency's most comfortable and attractive conference room for the occasion. There, over tea, coffee, and light refreshments, the attorneys and the protective services worker were all able to define the problems they perceived concerning the possibility of Diana taking back her child. They were encouraged by Mrs. Haley to express specifically what they wanted Diana to do to demonstrate to them that she was capable of being a good parent. In response, Diana told them all she was willing to do virtually anything they required to assure them of her fitness to care for her child again. An explicit plan was developed at the meeting: that Diana (1) visit Urban Day regularly to develop her parenting skills, (2) engage in regular, scheduled counseling with Mrs. Haley, (3) engage in psychotherapy with another psychotherapist two times a month, and (4) encourage the child's father to become involved in Dorothy's development. Diana and the father were not married but the young man was interested in becoming involved with the child.

Diana met all conditions. A little later, when new problems arose in her visitation schedule with the foster parents, Mrs. Haley organized a second problem-solving session at Urban Day addressing specific fears and designing a program to alleviate the problems. A visitation schedule was worked out that met everyone's approval. All this was accomplished by treating each person involved with respect and consideration, and by consciously creating an atmosphere of positive problem solving as opposed to the win–lose framework.

With these problem-solving meetings successfully accomplished, and Diana having met all requirements established by the meetings, Mrs. Haley assumed that Diana would be granted custody of her daughter, Dorothy, by the court at its next scheduled session involving her case. But what actually happened at the next court session was almost a repeat of the first, and perhaps a little more shocking because of the work done between times. The court ordered that Blue County retain custody and that Dorothy remain in foster care for at least another year. The reason given by the court was that "criteria for return of the child had not been met." In fact, the criteria had all been met. But the protective services social worker did not produce any of the necessary documentation in court.

Obviously, the guardian *ad litum*, the attorney for Blue County, and the protective services social worker had reverted to their original sense of power struggle over the case. Mrs. Haley learned later that the three attorneys and the Blue County worker had met together just prior to the court date, to settle things outside of court if possible. Instead, their adversarial perspectives resulted in another clash of wills. The agreements worked out so carefully in the sessions with Mrs. Haley were set aside. But no one informed Mrs. Haley or Diana Kinsman prior to the court appearance. Mrs. Haley was extremely disappointed in their actions as professionals, particularly in the social worker. Just as Mrs. Haley acts according to the framework of the code of ethics, she expects social work colleagues to act by it also. By disregarding explicit agreements with Diana Kinsman and Mrs. Haley, and by not informing them of her new intentions, the social worker for Blue County violated several sections of the code. These include at least the first three provisions under the respect, fairness, and courtesy principle, as explored earlier in this chapter.

In addition to violating the code of ethics, such behavior sets any client back in terms of his or her ability to trust other people, especially social workers, and to work in good faith. Avoiding such unpardonable damage to clients by social work professionals who have power over their lives is the major reason a code of ethics has been developed in the first place. Just because a person is a social worker does not mean that person will spontaneously act ethically and responsibly. Guidelines, and education as to what these guidelines are, are necessary for the personal and professional growth of the worker.

Mrs. Haley asserts that she will continue to work with the attorneys and the protective services worker in open problem-solving sessions if she possibly can. She admits that it is hard not to get pulled into the power struggle framework and to go behind the backs of the attorneys for Blue County as they did hers. Instead, she will consciously continue to work from an ethical frame of reference. She intends to ask for another meeting with all persons concerned before setting up a contest in court. She has every hope that she will be able to establish, through objective data gathered by Urban Day staff, Diana's readiness for parenting at this time. It must be admitted that Diana Kinsman is extremely lucky she developed a professional relationship with a committed worker like Mrs. Haley when she did. A less fortunate mother would be on her own at this point, with only a volatile court-appointed attorney to represent her side of the case, and under the win–lose framework that is not likely to be helpful for her. Without Mrs. Haley, Diana would probably settle into impotent cynicism after her recent experiences with the court. As it is, there is a good chance that Mrs. Haley will succeed in her interventions and help maintain her client's constructive efforts and self-esteem during the process.

Supervision and Evaluation

The last three provisions of the code concerning the social worker's responsibility to colleagues deal with supervision and evaluation. They are relatively straightforward. Provision nine states: "The social worker who serves as an employer, supervisor, or mentor to colleagues should make orderly and explicit arrangements regarding the conditions of their continuing professional relationship." Under this guideline, the employing or supervising social worker should make explicit such expectations as working hours, professional responsibilities, requirements for record keeping, schedule and objectives for supervision, and any other routine expectations required for acceptable work performance. These requirements will differ depending on the agency, its purpose, size, and the complexity of the staff.

Provision ten states that "the social worker who has the responsibility for employing and evaluating the performance of other staff members should fulfill such responsibility in a fair, considerate, and equitable manner, on the basis of clearly enunciated criteria." Provision eleven goes on to further specify that "the social worker who has the responsibility for evaluating the performance of employees, supervisees, or students should share evaluations with them."

At Urban Day, Mrs. Haley takes care that each member of her staff knows on what basis he or she will be evaluated, and that the criteria are explicit. They have been worked out over the years with input from all staff concerned. According to Mrs. Haley, she and her staff conduct informal evaluations mutually and on a regular basis. She believes that just as she has to know what her workers hold to be important, so do they have to know what she values and expects from them. Because there is a continual exchange of professional opinion concerning any staff evaluation of major practice decisions, the staff does in fact share much decision making. In that sense, Mrs. Haley views her "power" as "boss" as largely illusory. What is important, she feels, is understanding the job that needs to be done, and then finding the best way to do it. The workers in the social service department, including Mrs. Haley as director, consult with one another in order to carry out their responsibilities in the best possible way.

There is, however, a formal annual employee evaluation at Urban Day, and Mrs. Haley shares the written evaluation with each respective social service worker in a private conference. Similarly, for students who have field placements at Urban Day, each associated college or university provides evaluation forms which must be filled out and returned by Mrs. Haley. In each case she shares the evaluations with the students before sending the forms back to the relevant university. In some cases, university faculty coordinators visit the agency to meet jointly with the student and Mrs. Haley. Each of the academic social work programs involved have explicit criteria for student evaluations, and these are shared with students from the beginning of their placement at Urban Day.

One last provision concerning respect, fairness and courtesy needs to be acknowledged. Provision five states that "the social worker who replaces or is replaced by a colleague in professional practice should act with consideration for the interest, character, and reputation of that colleague."

At Urban Day, there has been little or no turnover among the full-time workers in the social service department during the past several years. In a sense, however, the students who are placed with the agency for a semester or an academic year are replacing workers. Sometimes they are assigned cases which other workers have previously managed. Under these circumstances the agency worker retains formal responsibility for the case, but his or her professional role shifts to one of consulting with the student worker as the student develops new skills. During the process, it is important for both student and community worker to act with special consideration for each other's interests.

One way this is facilitated is for the agency worker to introduce the student to the client family in person. One or several joint meetings with clients, as needed, can help to establish a smooth transition. But once the student begins working relatively alone on a new case, it might be easy, given the zeal of a new student, for him or her to criticize the community worker's past efforts. On the other hand, the experienced community worker might become quite critical of the student's initial and sometimes naive effors. Under these circumstances provision five could well apply at Urban Day. Student and community worker should air their points of view with each other and perhaps consult with Mrs. Haley to resolve their differences, rather than making mean and nasty remarks about one another to clients, coworkers, or other students. Protecting the interests and reputation of other workers can only lead to better cooperation among social workers and, if differences are worked out appropriately, should be in the best interest of clients as well.

DEALING WITH COLLEAGUES' CLIENTS

The social worker's responsibility to the clients of colleagues is also an ethical matter. On this point the code states: "Dealing with Colleagues'

Clients—The social worker has the responsibility to relate to the clients of colleagues with full professional consideration." This means that the responsibilities to the client enumerated in the code of ethics must apply to any work done with colleagues' clients as well as to work with one's own. The worker must act ethically toward clients as much due to professional responsibility toward colleagues as due to professional responsibility toward the clients themselves. This is required to uphold the reputation of the colleague and the social work profession as a whole.

The principle dealing with the clients of colleagues has three provisions. The first is that "the social worker should not solicit the clients of colleagues." At Urban Day, there is no motivation for soliciting the clients of others, since individual community workers have a great deal of input in choosing the clients with whom they wish to work. Besides, the social service workers work under a fixed salary system and receive no financial benefit for taking on additional cases. Clients are too poor to pay for services. There is no economic or other benefit for soliciting clients under these circumstances, so this is simply a nonissue at Urban Day. However, at other types of agencies, particularly private practice agencies where social workers are paid on a per-client basis, the issue of soliciting colleagues' clients can be very real indeed. Social workers should keep in mind that clients should never be solicited from colleagues for reasons of personal monetary gain.

Provision two of this principle states: "The social worker should not assume professional responsibility for the clients of another agency or colleague without appropriate communication with that agency or colleague." This guideline asserts that a social worker should not accept a case for further service, even a voluntary self-referral, if the client has received social work intervention elsewhere, without first communicating with the former agency or worker. Since social work intervention must also be kept confidential, as discussed earlier in Chapter 3, such communication with a former agency or worker requires explicit and written permission from the client. On occasion, a client will refuse to give such permission. In this circumstance the worker must assure the client that all such communication will be kept strictly confidential, and that it is required for best professional planning. Usually this will result in the client's giving the necessary permission. However, if the prospective new client continues to refuse permission, the code is clear in indicating that he or she should not be accepted for service.

There are many reasons for this. One is, of course, to show respect, fairness, and courtesy to a professional colleague. Social workers usually want to know when a former client has sought service elsewhere. If the former worker has referred the client, he or she will be pleased to know that the client has followed through. If, on the other hand, the client is seeking service elsewhere out of dissatisfaction with a former worker, it is important that the worker be aware of this. Only then can the former worker evaluate his or her intervention efforts to determine why the client might have chosen to move on. Another reason for contacting former workers is that they may be aware of important information that can make future work with the client more realistic and effective. Again, clients may be reluctant for new workers to learn what efforts have been made in their behalf in the past, but the code is clear that no new efforts should be undertaken without communication with former service providers.

Occasionally an Urban Day worker, in consultation with Mrs. Haley, reaches the decision that a given client's interests would best be served by transferring him or her to to another worker within the agency. This most commonly occurs if the client in question is not responding well to a given worker's efforts, and there is reason to believe the client's response might be better with another worker. If all parties agree, the transfer will be made and a detailed case plan will be drawn up in advance to try to rectify prior problems.

The code of ethics' final provision concerning dealing with colleagues' clients states: "The social worker who serves the clients of colleagues, during a temporary absence or emergency, should serve those clients with the same consideration as that afforded any client." At Urban Day, of course, the various workers cover for each other during illness or vacations. When vacations are planned in advance, the regular worker has the opportunity to brief the covering worker regarding current circumstances and any likely problems. Records are kept up to date for each case by the respective workers in case of unexpected absence. When a worker is ill or absent on vacation, covering workers will take telephone calls and messages, but normally leave the major decisions for the regular worker to make on return. In cases where emergency decisions are required, these normally are made in consultation between the overseeing worker and Mrs. Haley. In this way the best possible professional consideration can be taken into account.

In summary, this chapter has examined the social worker's ethical responsibility to colleagues, as outlined in the code of ethics. This section of the code includes two principles, respect, fairness, and courtesy, and dealing with colleagues' clients. The chapter illustrates how the concepts of respect, fairness, and courtesy should be applied to the social worker's treatment of colleagues and clients alike, and how the concept of colleague can be extended across interdisciplinary and professional boundaries.

REVIEW

Chapter 4 discusses the social worker's ethical responsibility to colleagues. Many of the ethical requirements social workers hold for their clients are also held for their colleagues, although these ethical responsibilities may not be as well known, for example, confidentiality. For purposes of review, the entire third section of the social work code of ethics is reproduced below:

THE SOCIAL WORKER'S ETHICAL RESPONSIBILITY TO COLLEAGUES

J. Respect, Fairness, and Courtesy. The social worker should treat colleagues with respect, courtesy, fairness, and good faith.
1. The social worker should cooperate with colleagues to promote professional interests and concerns.
2. The social worker should respect confidences shared by colleagues in the course of their professional relationships and transactions.
3. The social worker should create and maintain conditions of practice that facilitate ethical and competent professional performance by colleagues.
4. The social worker should treat with respect, and represent accurately and fairly, the qualifications, views, and findings of colleagues and use appropriate channels to express judgments on these matters.
5. The social worker who replaces or is replaced by a colleague in professional practice should act with consideration for the interest, character, and reputation of that colleague.
6. The social worker should not exploit a dispute between a colleague and employers to obtain a position or otherwise advance the social worker's interest.
7. The social worker should seek arbitration or mediation when conflicts with colleagues require resolution for compelling professional reasons.
8. The social worker should extend to colleagues of other professions the same respect and cooperation that is extended to social work colleagues.
9. The social worker who serves as an employer, supervisor, or mentor to colleagues should make orderly and explicit arrangements regarding the conditions of their continuing professional relationship.
10. The social worker who has the responsibility for employing and evaluating the performance of other staff members should fulfill such responsibility in a fair, considerate, and equitable manner, on the basis of clearly enunciated criteria.
11. The social worker who has the responsibility for evaluating the performance of employees, supervisees, or students should share evaluations with them.

K. Dealing with Colleagues' Clients. The social worker has the responsibility to relate to the clients of colleagues with full professional consideration.
1. The social worker should not solicit the clients of colleagues.
2. The social worker should not assume professional responsibility for the clients of another agency or a colleague without appropriate communication with that agency or colleague.
3. The social worker who serves the clients of colleagues during a temporary absence or emergency should serve those clients with the same consideration as that afforded any client.

STUDY QUESTIONS

1 The author describes how she decided to extend the meaning of the term "colleague" to include nonprofessional as well as professional coworkers, for purposes of interpretation of the code of ethics in daily practice. Why? What do you think about this interpretation?

2 How did social workers at Urban Day "cooperate with colleagues to promote professional interests and concerns?"

3 How did Mrs. Haley facilitate ethical professional performance by colleagues, for example, the community workers? Papa Martinez?

4 Why did Mrs. Haley object to the hiring of Bonnie Nichols? What does the author mean by the statement: "There is nothing in the code of ethics which protects the social worker from adverse reaction when behavior that follows agency procedures and ethical guidelines is perceived as threatening."

5 If Ms. Nichols does not succeed in performing her new role as Education Director at Urban Day in a satisfactory manner, what course of action would you follow if you were Mrs. Haley?

6 In context of the case of Diana and Dorothy Kinsman, how does the author demonstrate the need for a social work code of ethics?

7 How does Mrs. Haley implement the code of ethics in terms of her evaluation procedures with her staff? Her students? What responsibilities do students have with respect to evaluating their supervisors?

8 Why is it important for a social worker to communicate with prior social service providers before accepting a new client? How might this ethical requirement conflict with the principle guaranteeing confidentiality to clients? If such a dilemma should arise with a given client, how can the social worker attempt to resolve it?

5

The Social Worker's Ethical Responsibility to Employers and Employing Organizations

The new referral looked familiar to Mrs. Haley as she examined the case summary sheet supplied by Blue County Protective Services. It wasn't that she actually knew the family or the particular child involved. It was just that she had seen a number of similar referrals and fervently wished Urban Day had more options to offer in terms of intervention. The referral in question was the two-year-old son of an unmarried couple, a Hispanic mother and white father. Both parents were nineteen years of age. The father was in the process of finishing high school while the mother was subsisting on an Aid to Families with Dependent Children grant from the Blue County Department of Public Welfare. She had dropped out of high school shortly before the birth of the baby and was now living in a small apartment in a low income, run-down area of the city. She was receiving no financial or emotional support from her family since they viewed her as in disgrace for bearing a child out of wedlock. She also was receiving no financial or emotional support from the father of the child.

The little Anglo-Hispanic boy had been referred to Urban Day because of suspected delays in his speech and motor development. His condition had originally been brought to the attention of Blue County by a concerned neighbor, who felt that the child was being neglected and abused by his mother. Investigation revealed a frail little boy who didn't move around much for his age and seemed unable to speak coherently. So severe was his apparent speech problem that protective services feared the boy might be retarded. However, because there was no visible evidence of intentional abuse, that is, no bruises or lacerations, the court did not order foster care. Instead it ordered referral to Urban Day for evaluation and further court review in six months. The referral sheet from Blue County Protective Services described the boy as neglected physically and emotionally and commented that there appeared to be a lack of maternal bonding.

In Mrs. Haley's opinion, derived from many years of practice, it made little sense to attempt to strengthen maternal bonding via a program that required full-day attendance at Urban Day. Such a program separated child and mother for too many hours. This child's delays were probably the result of inadequate *parenting* by a depressed, lonely, and unskilled young woman *and* an absent man. A more effective treatment plan in her opinion would involve half days for the child at Urban Day along with training in parental skills for the mother and outreach to the father. But, as noted previously, Urban Day did not offer half-day programming and home-training money had run out. Nor were teachers allocated time or space to work with parents at the center.

Then came another familiar case, an infant girl only a few months old, born with cystic fibrosis. The center rarely handled cases involving cystic fibrosis. The unhappily familiar part was that the parents, a black working-class couple, were devoted spouses and caring parents. They wanted the best for their little girl. But since they were not abusing parents, they might have to be referred to a half-day program not nearly so effective or personal as Urban Day. If Urban Day had a half-day option, it could take these types of children, who needed a good deal of skilled intervention to alleviate their physical problems but whose home situation was nurturant and safe.

COMMITMENTS TO EMPLOYING ORGANIZATIONS

What do the above two examples have to do with the social worker's commitment to the employing organization? They help illustrate that the kind of practice a social worker can perform is very much dependent on the policies and procedures of the employing organization. Social work practice and social welfare agency policy are not separate issues. They are very much intertwined. Mrs. Haley could not plan for the little Anglo-Hispanic boy to spend half days at Urban Day if the agency was unable to offer such a program. In some cases carrying out agency policy can create an ethical dilemma for a social worker if that policy is not in the best interests of certain types of clients.

According to the code of ethics, the social worker's responsibility to employers and employing organizations is: "Commitment to Employing Organization—The social worker should adhere to commitments made to the employing organization." According to the code, then, the social worker is ethically responsible for meeting the position requirements specified in the agency's job description when the worker is hired. Therefore, it is important for the worker to understand what a given job will entail before accepting it. Sometimes a job description includes a written list of expectations and responsibilities. At other times, the job description is verbal. In the latter case, it is a good idea for the prospective employee to take notes regarding job responsibilities during or shortly after the initial interview and to review them in detail with the prospective employer before accepting the position. In this way misunderstandings are minimized.

Another good idea is to ask the prospective employer detailed questions regarding job expectations during the interview. These might include the type of work to be done, the size of the work load, the supervision and training opportunities provided, and the working hours. It is easy to overlook important details in the often pressured setting of the employment interview where the major question in the anxious applicant's mind usually is, "Will I get the job?" In a time when jobs are scarce, it may seem that nothing matters except impressing the interviewer and securing the work; any position that comes with a regular paycheck will do. But even when a steady income is urgently needed, it can become impossible to retain a job at an agency where existing policies are incompatible with competent ethical practice. Hence it is important to choose one's place of employment as carefully as possible to be sure, before accepting a job, that one can live with the agency's basic purpose, policies, and procedures.

The social worker who accepts employment at an agency where commitments made to the employing organization do not seem to be in the best interests of clients is faced with an ethical dilemma. One's ethical responsibility to the employing organization violates one's responsibility to clients, and vice versa. If the social worker clearly perceives that commitments made to a prospective employer will violate client interests, it is far better to refuse a job at the outset. Not only does this avert an ethical dilemma, but making clear the reasons for turning down a position is one way, albeit small, that an agency may be influenced to change its policies.

Mrs. Haley, for example, has reservations about the ethics of accepting the position of social worker at one of the largest agencies for handicapped people in Project City. This agency deals with handicapped people from infancy through old age, and the clientele is much larger than Urban Day's. Yet the social service staff consists of one person. Mrs. Haley has learned from experience that none of the clients she refers to this agency receive social services. The worker there is simply overwhelmed with referrals, and most potential clients get lost. Clients referred to the agency who do not appear on their own simply vanish into the vast anonymity of the inner city; there is absolutely no time for the social worker to do any sort of outreach. Hence Mrs. Haley now refuses to refer clients to this agency and believes that accepting the job of social worker there may violate professional ethics because simply holding the position enables the agency to profess that it provides social services when in fact it does not.

Since the code of ethics requires social workers to honor commitments made to the employing organization, it is very important that prospective employees understand the setting where they are applying for employment. Is the purpose of the agency genuinely beneficial to society, in the social worker's perception? For example, is helping provide early education to young handicapped children an ethically sound purpose? If so, do the agency policies and procedures seem compatible with its purpose? Does the job description seem reasonable, given the nature of the setting and the clientele served? If so, then one can probably accept employment without the risk of serious ethical dilemmas.

Improving Agency Policy

Once a social worker is employed, the code of ethics notes: "The social worker should work to improve the employing agency's policies and procedures, and the efficiency and effectiveness of its services." Improving agency policy and procedure is, of course, a big order. Everyone is aware of the not-so-funny joke about how impossible it is in a bureaucracy to change so much as a comma on an application form. Once agency policies and procedures are established, they have a tendency to become rigid. Of course, one's position at the agency can make a real difference with respect to influencing policy. Those with supervisory responsibilities generally have more power to affect policy decisions than direct service workers, for example. But the code of ethics does not exhort supervisors or administrators only to improve agency policy and procedures, it exhorts all social workers to try to do so.

"And let it begin with me," might be a good motto for a social worker. For example, Mrs. Haley takes it upon herself to keep up with recent research pertaining to handicapped children. Awareness of the latest developments in this area allows her to do the best possible work for her clients, including the advocacy of change in agency policy. Mrs. Haley was fortunate to have been hired by the agency in which she received her graduate training, so that she was already familiar with many of the issues and concerns regarding handicapped children and families trapped by poverty and/or ethnic minority status. But many social workers are hired by agencies quite different from the ones in which they were trained. In these cases, workers should be responsible not only to themselves but to their agency to educate themselves fully regarding its major issues and concerns, so that they can participate in efforts to improve services.

In accord with the "and let it begin with me" perspective, Mrs. Haley also recently reviewed her own office procedures. She decided she needed to become more efficient. An alarming amount of paper had begun to pile up on her desk. This was in part because of her open-door policy, an otherwise admirable practice that meant that she was readily available to staff and clients who happened to stop by with problems. This policy led to excellent rapport and high responsiveness to immediate staff and client needs—and noticeable tardiness in paperwork. A cheerful little plaque on her desk announced, "a clean uncluttered desk is the sign of a sick mind." No need to worry about compulsive behavior here! But gradually, insidiously, the little piles of notes and slips and forms became terrifying. Something had to be done.

So Mrs. Haley decided to review her priorities. Responsiveness to staff and clients and availability to meet immediate needs were high on her list, but she realized paperwork was important, too. Those papers were required by public schools so that "graduating" Urban Day clients could be accepted into city special education programs; they were required by former treatment agencies so that Urban Day could receive necessary records; they were required by parents whose permission was necessary to have educational records transferred. Yes, the paperwork had to be done, too, or the best interests of clients wouldn't be served. So Mrs. Haley decided to modify her open-door policy and experiment with some other office reforms.

Part of her experimentation involved establishing a time for herself when she wasn't available to anyone. Mrs. Haley put aside the first half hour of every working day to plan, to lay out priorities. To help with planning, she obtained three layered filing trays and placed them on her desk, labeling them "long-term," "intermediate," and "short-term." She then could sort out her paperwork according to its urgency and, as a reward, was able to view a grand expanse of clean desk. She developed a system whereby she could handle each piece of paper only twice—once when she placed it in the appropriate tray and again when she removed it from the tray to complete it and route it on its way. This allowed her to complete her paperwork quickly and efficiently.

In addition to the half hour set aside each morning, Mrs. Haley also set aside another two hours per day to complete paperwork and undertake regular case reviews. This made it possible for Mrs. Haley to improve her services to clients by improved planning, thereby avoiding continual crisis intervention.

Mrs. Haley's new office policies and procedures did make her less accessible. Regular clients now needed to make appointments, and staff sometimes had to wait to see her when they wanted to consult her about certain cases. There were, however, some unexpected and quite beneficial side effects. Mrs. Haley's staff weaned itself of a dependency she hadn't fully recognized before. They began to make decisions on their own under circumstances in which they previously would have turned to her for advice. They learned to value and trust their own casework assessments more.

Thus, through innovation and experimentation, Mrs. Haley introduced a number of procedural changes in her own office policy. Some worked, while others were too cumbersome and were dropped; but all the efforts and changes demonstrated that individual workers can and should be responsible to evaluate and improve their own work performance, policies, and procedures.

Organizing in-service training is another means by which social workers can work to improve agency policy and procedures. In-service sessions can be instrumental in the education of both staff and formal policymakers alike concerning unmet client needs. Such sessions generally educate in a nonthreatening manner that can encourage dialogue leading to change. Mrs. Haley, as noted before, has used in-service sessions to alert the agency to the special needs of burn victims, single parents, battered women, and culturally deprived families.

Another way to affect agency policy is simply to discuss it with the appropriate staff and administrators. Every agency has a formal authority structure. There are people "on top" who have the right to make policy decisions. Persuading them of the need for changes can be effective if they are approached in the right way, which will differ from agency to agency. Perhaps there are informal channels of influence. Some individuals at lower levels have power because they are particularly liked or respected. Perhaps certain persons in authority are more open to being approached by those beneath them than others. Some people like to be approached in person first. Others prefer a written memo or proposal.

Mrs. Haley feels particularly fortunate that she works for a small, flexible agency with an administration that listens to its staff. Staff are welcome to discuss their ideas in person with the administrators. As the case involving the hiring of Bonnie Nichols suggests, all is not perfect at Urban Day. Open disagreement with administrative decisions can indeed bring discomfort and threats. This, however, is true almost everywhere, because people are only too human. Threatened sanctions certainly can inhibit staff willingness to express opinions openly. But at Urban Day, under normal circumstances, the administration values and seeks out staff input on agency policy and procedures. For this reason, Mrs. Haley can live with the imperfections of Urban Day that she perceives.

"Sure," she says, "I work for an agency that doesn't have enough parental involvement. But I'm working for an agency that's working towards more. So I'm right within my value system." This value system, and the ethical behavior arising from it, requires a great deal of problem analysis and intervention efforts beyond simply working with the clients themselves. For example, before Urban Day could provide more parental involvement, its staff had to become capable of working with parents. But the teachers were professionally trained only to work with children. What to do? Who had time or money to go back to school, and what program taught teachers how to work with parents? So Mrs. Haley took the time to interest and involve teachers in working with parents and to gain the skills to do it. She involved other competent staff members in this effort. For example, she arranged for teachers to observe the physical and occupational therapists working with parents through the agency's one-way mirror system. As the skills and confidence of the teachers improved, they voluntarily began to increase their work with parents. And they derived some benefits for themselves as well, which encouraged further efforts. After all, if parents can, for example, assist in toilet training their children at home, that can only make the teachers' job in the classroom easier.

In the past year, many positive changes have occurred at Urban Day with respect to parents. Staff acceptance of the presence of parents at the center has increased. Now it is seen as an opportunity rather than a distraction. Many parents come in every day, even those from families that could be classified as "multiproblem." A difficulty that continues to exist is that agency policy still doesn't officially reflect the fact that teachers put in a lot of time working with parents. No special time or extra staff is scheduled for this activity largely because this would involve increased expense. But at least the agency administration now informally encourages staff to work with parents; teachers are free to do so in any way they can.

Home training for parents is another area that Mrs. Haley, along with other staff, has urged the agency to strengthen. For a time Urban Day had grant funds specifically for this activity, but when those funds expired the work lapsed. Now Mrs. Haley has been able to allocate a good proportion of the time of Mrs. Gantz, one of her community workers, to this activity. Home training helps expand the skills of the parents in working with their own children, just as parent work by the teachers does in the classroom setting. Research demonstrates that the one-to-one approach is extremely effective with young children, and that parents can be effective teachers for their children. One must be careful, however, not to overvalue even such a fine and family-oriented concept as home training to the extent of recommending it as the treatment of choice for all. The best approach to working with a given child depends tremendously on the circumstances of that child and the respective family.

Home training as a concept assumes that a parent has the knowledge, skills, and desire to do this sort of work. And working with handicapped children *is* work, an extremely important sort of work that can avert all sorts of more serious problems later for both the child and society. Home training for the handicapped assumes that at least one parent has time, is present in the home a number of hours during the day, and has the proper information and motivation. It also assumes the parent has worked out most of his or her feelings toward handicapped children in general, and toward the special circumstance of bearing a handicapped child. In addition, the parent needs a support system to work with to provide encouragement and feedback. Most parents served by an agency like Urban Day are themselves handicapped by poverty, racism, and sexism, and thus many of these factors are absent. It is possible that the best method for encouraging normal development of many children is a specialized center with skilled staff trained to do the job, along with training for parents. A center can ideally provide not only specialized treatment for the children but also for the parents, including guidance and support.

Mrs. Haley has learned from experience that developing bonding between an abusing parent and a handicapped child can be extremely difficult. It is especially difficult when the child is removed from the home five full days per week, and as a result she has urged the development of more options for intervention at Urban Day. Others have also wanted to work in this direction, given their own knowledge and experience. There has been disagreement about the options desirable, but an openness to discussing change has always existed. Funding has, however, been a major limiting factor. If, for example, Urban Day were to develop a half-day treatment option, twice as much busing might be required. Who would pay for it?

A great deal of effort has been expended in an attempt to devise solutions. Several have recently been implemented. For example, certain children are now being accepted for treatment for two or three full days per week only. This allows more children to be served, and permits part-time service to some children who could benefit by such an arrangement. It also allows the agency to compete for funds more effectively under the guidelines of the major funding body, the Combined Community Services Board. Some handicapped children from nonabusing families are once again being referred to Urban Day. Children with bonding issues can be allowed to spend certain days at home, to help maintain emotional connection with the mother. Home training and outpatient occupational therapy, physical therapy, and speech therapy have been made more available. The agency's overall requirement for busing has not been increased by these extra options. These are truly innovative approaches to a set of problems that are not only treatment-related but administrative. Given its short history, the agency can be genuinely proud of its adaptibility both to human need and to economic circumstance.

In spite of Urban Day's current progress, Mrs. Haley continues to perceive needed changes and to disagree with some agency policies. She believes that a critical stance with respect to agency policy and procedure is not only her right but her responsibility to both the agency and the profession. Mrs. Haley believes that the age-old argument of ends versus means is relevant here, and she believes strongly that the ends can never justify the means. "We can choose only the means," she points out very simply. "So we must choose the means that seem the most right. We can then only hope the intended ends will follow."

Mrs. Haley's position is arguable, but if one accepts her supposition that human beings truly *do* have the power only to choose the means, certain consequences are inevitable. Mrs. Haley cannot ignore what she perceives as poor agency policy and procedure (the means) for the apparently benevolent "end" of permitting a well-meaning agency to continue without the painfulness of rocking the boat. To permit inadequate or undesirable "means" to continue would be professionally unethical. Her beliefs are strongly supported by the particular guideline of the social work code of ethics dealt with in this section, which we will quote again here for emphasis: "The social worker should work to improve the employing agency's policies and procedures, and the efficiency and effectiveness of its service."

Discrimination Issues

"Really," Sally Brown said. Sally was a long-term teacher at Urban Day, highly respected for her dedication and hard work. "I don't want to take the new infants' classroom. I very much prefer working with the older children, the ones that can give you a little more response. Please, I know we need another classroom for infants, but I'd rather keep my present age group. Besides, I don't have any infants at all in my classroom now and taking the new room would mean I'd have to break my relationship with all the kids I'm currently working with."

"Really," George said. George was a very new teacher at Urban Day, already prized by staff and administration. Not only was he a good teacher, but his arrival had helped improve the ratio of male teachers at Urban Day from zero in four to one in four. He was personable and added a welcome masculine presence to classroom and playground. "Really," George said. "I don't want to take the new infants' classroom. I very much prefer working with the older children, the ones that can give you a little more response. Please, I know we need a new classroom for infants, but I'd rather keep my present age group. Besides, I've only one infant in my classroom now, and taking the new room would mean I'd have to break my relationship with all but one of the kids I'm currently working with."

Who should have to take the new infant's classroom? The teacher who had been at Urban Day the longest and would have to break her relationship with all her former children? Or the new teacher who would be able to maintain his relationship with at least one child? Usually seniority lends weight to one's preference at an agency where at least two competent people want a new position or, as in this case, where two competent people *don't* want a new position. What had happened at Urban Day was that an influx of infant referrals were requiring a temporary shift in classroom organization. One of the two rooms for toddlers would have to be temporarily used as a room for infants.

An impartial judicial body would probably decide in favor of Sally. George should have to take on the new classroom. George had less seniority and was already working with one of the children slated for the new room. Moreover, as may be recalled from a previous anecdote, Sally had a special interest in artwork which could best be employed with the toddler age group. But impartial justice did not prevail in this case: Sally was required to take on the job. Why? Because Sally was a woman, and after all, "everyone knows" women know what to do with babies. Everyone simply expected that Sally would work more effectively with the infants. Moreover, the administration probably worried more about losing George than they did about Sally. George had less investment in the agency and more job mobility. Male teachers for very young children are hard to find.

This common, everyday occurrence demonstrates what sexism means in the world of work. Sexism means that women usually have fewer choices than men in terms of the job market, and that their preferences at work are not honored as often, even if they have more seniority and experience, and even within a small, very personal agency like Urban Day. The structure of Urban Day also reflects sexism. Almost the entire staff is female; the top administrator is male. The particular male on the top, the agency director, is highly qualified, experienced, and productive. He merits his position without question. But how does it happen that in so many agencies the top administrators are qualified men? Why aren't there more qualified women? And what happens to the women who are just as qualified? Why don't they move up, too? In social work agencies, statistics prove that given the same education and years of service, men are much more likely than women to move into top administrative positions.

The purpose of this book with regard to sex and racial discrimination is limited to illustrating how sexism and racism are manifested in one high quality, minority-conscious agency. Even our best organizations tend to mirror conditions in the rest of society. It is important for young men and women to recognize the type of society we live in so that all can work to make it more equitable.

Just as Urban Day mirrors the sexism in American society, it also mirrors the racism. Many ethnic minority employees hold jobs at Urban Day, but almost all hold the low-level positions, those of child-care worker or custodial aide. Looking at the overall employee structure, one can see clear effects of both racism and sexism. The lowest positions are generally held by women of ethnic minority status. Next come the white women. White women have achieved academic training for service occupations such as social worker, teacher, and therapist, and thus can hold profession-al positions within the agency. Professional women's jobs in the United States generally tend to extend the nurturant role socially required of females within the family setting into the broader world of paid work. Urban Day is no exception. At Urban Day, however, women also hold the lower administrative positions. This is a result of its relatively liberal stance and the fact that it is a service-oriented agency most of whose employees are female. Mrs. Haley, for example, is director of the social service department. Above her, the program director is also a woman. But above all the professional white women on the staff stands the agency director, a white male.

What does the social work code of ethics have to say about issues of discrimination, such as sexism and racism? Provision three under the principle of the code dealing with commitments to employing organizations, states unequivocally: "The social worker should act to prevent and eliminate discrimination in the employing organization's work assignments and in its employment policies and practices." A tall order indeed!

At Urban Day, Mrs. Haley indicated her interest in discrimination early in her employment, so the agency appointed her to be the affirmative-action officer. She then undertook a variety of efforts to improve the situation. As a first step she hoped to attract minorities into professional positions at Urban Day. She also hoped to attract more males. She made it clear that she viewed affirmative action as not only a social work responsibility but an obligation of the agency as a whole. Fortunately, administrators at Urban Day value affirmative action in behavior as well as words, and they agreed to support Mrs. Haley's efforts. When she sought out minority newspapers and professional publications, and began to advertise job openings in these sources, Urban Day was willing to pay the bill.

This campaign has had some results, attracting minority applicants for some of the professional positions. But few of the ethnic minority applicants have possessed the required certification and skills. The needs of the handicapped children and the requirements of the accrediting and funding bodies of importance to Urban Day have precluded taking on staff who lack formal qualifications. Gradually, Mrs. Haley has realized that there are few minority persons who are qualified for the professional jobs Urban Day has to offer. Society is not training them. Which is one reason, of course, why the agency structure mirrors society as a whole. People can't develop their skills if society does not provide them with an opportunity to do so.

Just as Mrs. Haley has been unable to find many qualified minority candidates for the professional positions at Urban Day, she has also been unable to find many men (except for the custodial staff). Men tend to select themselves out of child-care-oriented positions in advance, viewing them as female professions, just as women tend to select themselves *in* in disproportionate numbers. Again, is this society's fault or a matter of individual choice? Obviously, such a question confuses rather than clarifies the issue. The "fault" is not a matter of "either–or" but rather of "both–and." Most people tend to try to become what they think others will esteem, so personal choice and societal pressures are involved simultaneously.

Mrs. Haley now views affirmative action at Urban Day as an evolving orientation and set of behavioral practices rather than a single goal. The means for recruiting more minority and male employees are continually adjusted and refined with experience. She continues to advertise all job openings in minority newspapers and other ethnic publications. She also makes as much use of word-of-mouth advertisement as possible and takes pains to make her staff aware of the agency's affirmative-action goals. She actively seeks minority and male interns in an effort to assist with the training of future minority professionals. Although he has since left, Mrs. Haley was able to recruit a male social worker for her staff at one point. Later, she recruited an ethnic minority staff person, Mrs. Dillon.

The code of ethics guideline, "The social worker should act to prevent and eliminate discrimination in the employing organization's work assignments and in its employment policies and practices," can apply to an agency as a whole, as discussed above. It can also be applied to a particular department. Mrs. Haley makes sure that work assignments within her own department are fair. The social service department is the place at Urban Day where she can have the most direct and immediate influence, so that is the place she begins demonstrating her ethical orientation. Mrs. Haley makes sure that her staff members have input concerning the kind of cases they prefer. Staff members recognize that they have particular strengths and weaknesses, and so they request particular types of cases where possible.

For example, Mrs. Dillon is very strong in her knowledge of community resources. She prefers to use a self-help-oriented approach with clients who can take her information and follow up on it themselves. Mrs. Dillon achieved her own position through dogged perseverance and hard work, and so she has a difficult time being patient with clients who won't do things for themselves.

But Carol Jean Heintz loves clients who need to be taken under her motherly wing. She is willing to expend extraordinary efforts working with unmotivated clients. She views clients who don't try as being *unable* to help themselves, rather than as unwilling. To Carol Jean go the cases no one else feels much hope for.

Mrs. Gantz, as explained previously, was originally hired at Urban Day as a home trainer. She, not surprisingly, prefers clients who can benefit from specific tutoring in the home. Mrs. Gantz has extensive and up-to-date knowledge regarding pertinent readings and resources in child development.

Mrs. Haley generally takes on whatever cases the others don't happen to select. She feels she is best at working with clients who have communication disorders. For example, many clients from multiproblem backgrounds have received so many mixed messages from significant others during their lives that they have lost the ability to distinguish reality. The words they have heard haven't matched voice tone, eye contact, or body language so they are likely to respond to the wrong things. They need to do some reality testing, some checking out of who they are and what is happening to them.

Of course there are times when caseloads vary enough in size that the one with the lightest load takes on the next referral regardless of its apparent characteristics. If difficulties then occur, staff will consult together. As a last resort, cases may be transferred to a more appropriate worker or to Mrs. Haley. Through seeking and responding to ongoing staff input, Mrs. Haley can assure that arbitrary discrimination in work assignments is avoided within her own department.

Agency Resources

The next provision in this section of the code of ethics states: "The social worker should use with scrupulous regard, and only for the purpose for which they are intended, the resources of the employing organization." The meaning of this guideline is straightforward. The social worker is to treat agency resources with care and use them only for specified agency business.

Urban Day certainly has resources which could be abused. For example, as discussed earlier, the agency has a car which workers can sign out to transport clients. Conceivably, a worker could sign the car out to take a joy ride in the country! For that matter, agency *time* is a resource. Workers are expected to use agency time for agency work, not cruising the countryside or doing their family shopping. The agency also has many donated clothing supplies. Sometimes the clothes donated are for adults and these, of course, are not the right size for the agency children. Staff may buy these clothes but may not take them for free. The money is put into the parent fund. In addition, donated items that are not appropriate for young children are sold in rummage sales conducted by the parents' group, and the money received is likewise put into the parent fund for speakers, needed equipment, and the like.

Rather than abusing agency resources, most staff members are more likely to augment them. For example, staff members frequently donate clothes to meet the needs of a particular child for whom the existing supplies are not quite appropriate. They also donate their time outside of work hours to care for children in emergencies. For example, in one recent case a client's mother had to be hospitalized for emergency surgery. No other family member was available who could care for the little deaf child, a two-year-old boy who spent his days at Urban Day. Two or three of the Urban Day staff took turns caring for the boy in their own homes after work, including Mrs. Haley, who could communicate with him in rudimentary sign language. Obviously, this type of service is not required by the code of ethics. But it is the kind of service inspired by Urban Day, or perhaps its tiny clients or their frequently overburdened parents.

Since the world is never perfect, staff members occasionally become aware of others who are abusing resources in some minor way. For example, not long ago a staff member took some ailing plants home from the lobby to nurse them back to health. In the process, the voluntary caretaker became attached to the plants, and she didn't immediately return them when they were once again healthy. Another staff member, while visiting her, saw the plants in her home and reminded her of their origin. The plants were returned. As Mrs. Haley explains it, "If any one of us becomes aware of an abuse of resources, we feel a responsibility to say something, even if it's a little embarrassing at the time. It's like we're a family in a way. If your little brother wastes all the breakfast cereal, you ask him to stop it and explain why."

Urban Day, then, doesn't experience much abuse of resources. Rather, staff themselves actually contribute needed supplies and personal time. Mrs. Haley's own staff perhaps donates more time than most; various members and the student interns regularly babysit during parents' meetings, for example. Mrs. Haley says she never goes out of her way to check up on her staff. She accepts where they say they are going and records without question the mileage they report having driven for agency business. She believes she has everything to gain by trusting her staff, and that they would have everything to lose if they were not trustworthy. Mrs. Haley simply expects adherence to high principles and excellent work from her staff. That frame of reference, from her conscious perspective, doesn't give permission for anything else to occur. And her experience suggests that the Urban Day staff avoids abusing agency resources and will personally bring any perceived abuse to a violator's attention.

NASW Concerns

One other provision under the principle dealing with responsibility to employing organizations should be noted here. Provision two states: "The social worker should not accept employment or arrange student field placements in an organization which is currently under public sanction by NASW for violating personnel standards, or imposing limitations on or penalties for professional actions on behalf of clients."

What this provision is referring to is the practice where social workers who feel their professional rights and responsibilities have been violated or ignored by their employing agencies can request that the National Association of Social Workers review their cases. This is one of the specific ways social workers can mobilize external pressure upon their agencies in the interest of reform. But what if the NASW accepts the case and then, after review, agrees that the worker's professional rights have been violated by the agency? The only way *it* can then apply pressure is by making the matter public and requesting NASW members to refuse employment there, pending a resolution of the issue at hand. NASW sanctions bear weight only if respected by other social workers; hence this specific guideline has been written into the code of ethics. Upholding professional ethics, therefore, involves boycotting any agency under NASW sanction. Needless to say, Urban Day is not under NASW sanction; in fact, several schools of social work have used it as a training agency for student interns in the past few years.

In summary, this chapter has explored and illustrated the social worker's ethical responsibility to employers and employing organizations. The chapter has demonstrated the intertwined relationship between policy and practice, using specific case examples to illustrate how effective social work practice can only be conducted in settings where enlightened policy permits. The social worker must honor commitments made to the employing organization, but at the same time, the practitioner must also work toward improving agency policy and procedures. Improvement should begin with the worker's own particular policy and procedures and develop from there.

REVIEW

This chapter has examined the portion of the social work code of ethics dealing with the social worker's ethical responsibility to employers and employing organizations. To assist the student in integration and review, the entire fourth heading of the code will be outlined below.

THE SOCIAL WORKER'S ETHICAL RESPONSIBILITY TO EMPLOYERS AND EMPLOYING ORGANIZATIONS

L. Commitments to Employing Organization. The Social Worker should adhere to commitments made to the employing organization.
    1. The social worker should work to improve the employing agency's policies and procedures, and the efficiency and effectiveness of its services.
    2. The social worker should not accept employment or arrange student field placements in an organization which is currently under public sanction by NASW for violating personnel standards, or imposing limitations on or penalties for professional actions on behalf of clients.
    3. The social worker should act to prevent and eliminate discrimination in the employing organization's work assignments and in its employment policies and practices.
    4. The social worker should use with scrupulous regard, and only for the purpose for which they are intended, the resources of the employing organization.

STUDY QUESTIONS

1 What do the case examples involving the Anglo-Hispanic two-year-old boy and the little black girl with cystic fibrosis have to do with the social worker's ethical responsibility toward the employing organization?

2 Why is it important for the social worker considering a job at a prospective agency of employment to understand the agency's basic purpose, policies, and procedures before accepting the job?

3 In what ways can "improving agency policy and procedure" begin with oneself? In what ways did Mrs. Haley strive to improve her own policies and procedures?

4 In what ways did Mrs. Haley endeavor to effect agency policies and procedures at Urban Day through change from within?

5 How is racism and sexism evident at Urban Day? What factors in society help maintain these circumstances? In ourselves as individuals? How does Mrs. Haley attempt to combat racism and sexism at Urban Day?

6 How does Mrs. Haley avoid discrimination in work assignments within her own department?

7 In what ways are Urban Day staff respectful of agency resources? How do they augment them at times?

The Social Worker's Ethical Responsibility to the Social Work Profession

"Well, and what do you do?" the lawyer asked me very politely as we strode together across the arid lands of southern Utah. He was wearing jeans, boots, and a white cowboy hat; he really was. My sister told me it was the first time she had ever seen him out of a three-piece suit. But we were all camping together this weekend—some twenty-odd children and nearly as many parents and assorted relatives including one aunt, me. It was the final fling for the graduating class of sixth graders, and the children and adults were enjoying themselves and getting to know one another better.

"I'm a social worker," I answered, as I now usually make a point to do. I didn't used to. I used to go out of my way to say that I worked with retarded children, older people, the emotionally disturbed, foster families, or whatever the case was at the time. Later I might say that I was a teacher. I would add "social work" quite softly if further pressed, hoping that would end the conversation because I was afraid the next words out of my questioner's mouth would be something like, "Oh, but isn't that depressing? And you don't make very much money, do you?" Growing eloquent, the person might then suggest that, low pay notwithstanding, I was the cause of the national budget deficit. And then I would feel, for some reason, that I needed to apologize. The absurd myths we live with. They do affect us, our personal lives as well as our professional ones. Societal priorities do change, and sometimes they undermine social welfare efforts, as they have over the past few years. People who work professionally in social welfare fields, then, have had added to the burden of their difficult work the burden of society's lack of appreciation and understanding.

Anyway, to continue. I no longer hide what I am, because I feel there is a message I need to communicate. I want people to know that I am a social worker, that I personally represent what a social worker is like, and that I believe in what my profession stands for.

"Well, well," my friend replied. "Isn't that rather depressing? And you can't make much money at it, can you?" He tactfully left out the part about the budget deficit. "Now I really enjoy my job," he said. "I create financial packages that allow new businesses to get their start, and I can practically guarantee them success from the beginning, because of the kind of financing arrangements I can put together. I help create jobs this way, you see, so that people who are really deserving can pull themselves up by their bootstraps." In this way he let me know he was socially responsible too, probably more than I was.

In days of yore I might have smiled sweetly and complimented him and wandered off into the cactus plants to be by myself in peace. Now I smiled sweetly and complimented him sincerely for the creativity he clearly was proud of. "Yes," I continued, "and in a way social work is very much like the work you do. Social workers have to be amazingly creative to assist people to find and sort through options they may have not been aware of before. Sometimes people are quite capable of solving the problems they come to us with by themselves, only they don't know enough about the resources available to them. One of our jobs is to help them get in touch with these resources." I was carefully using familiar terms like creativity and resources.

"Humph," the lawyer answered. There was a moment or so of silence. Then he continued: "You know, I just don't understand parents who won't take care of their children and so they go to people like you to do it for them. I just can't understand how people can be like that. I guess they must be just—well—irresponsible or something. Now don't you find working with people like that depressing, knowing they're not much good and are never going to change?"

"Well," I answered truthfully, "if I really believed people wouldn't change even with new information and options, then I might get depressed, and of course social workers get depressed sometimes. It's a tough profession, and underfunded so that caseloads are often too high and burnout is a real problem. But often our job is exciting too. We assess the problems brought to us and help our clients sort through potential solutions so that they can take constructive steps themselves to improve their situations."

"Oh," said the lawyer, and his eyes began to glaze. Too much too fast, I realized. He hadn't heard what he expected to hear and couldn't take it in. These were supposed to be social pleasantries we were exchanging, not thoughts and ideas that might conflict. Better to ease off for a while and return to the small talk. But I hoped he would remember later on that he had met a social worker who took pride in the profession. As for me, I rewarded myself by secretly patting myself on the back for trying, because there clearly wasn't going to be a reward from outside myself this time. Perhaps if I meet the man again in the future, I'll be able to find another appropriate opportunity to challenge his stereotypes. The next time or the time after that he might be able to hear me.

MAINTAINING THE INTEGRITY OF THE PROFESSION

The fifth major heading of the social work code of ethics addresses the social worker's ethical responsibility to the profession. The first principle in this section states: "Maintaining the Integrity of the Profession—The social worker should uphold and advance the values, ethics, knowledge, and mission of the profession."

Most social workers have little difficulty believing in the major values of the profession, its mission, or the ethics as outlined in this code. And we spend a good part of our lives honestly searching to improve our knowledge so that we can be better practitioners. The difficulty lies more in upholding these values, ethics, knowledge, and mission. This can be a real challenge if the word upholding is interpreted to mean not just practicing according to their guidelines but actually explaining and advancing them to non-social workers. And that is precisely how the code of ethics defines "uphold" when it states in the first provision under this principle: "The social worker should protect and enhance the dignity and integrity of the profession and should be responsible and vigorous in discussion and criticism of the profession."

Being "responsible and vigorous in discussion and criticism of the profession" requires not only careful thought but also a willingness to stand up and be counted. Because social work is a controversial profession, it is often easier to sit back and keep quiet. Why is social work a controversial profession? While there are many possible answers to this question, the simplest probably has to do with the fact that we are conceived to work with the "down and out," which, among others, we do. And who are the "down and out" but "losers," people who can't or won't help themselves and therefore must be inherently an inferior breed? The result is guilt by association; working with losers taints us as losers, too. Worse, we can't help our clients anyway since there must be something wrong with them; otherwise they wouldn't be losers!

To complicate matters, social workers often do work with the losers in society. This is certainly true at Urban Day. The majority of Urban Day's clientele cluster at the lower end of the socioeconomic scale. Many of them suffer major physical and mental handicaps; and so they are, in truth, from a certain point of view, demonstrably "inferior." They truly cannot use their bodies or their minds as well as "normal" people can. What kind of people would want to help "losers" like these? Well, social workers, among others. But why? The commitment to invest major energy in people who are not making it on their own is unusual in this society, and even the motivation to do so is suspect to others. Social workers are put down for being "bleeding hearts," for example. Or, stated in a different way, anyone who would want to do what social workers do must be soft in the head.

Mrs. Haley, in a passionate exchange with another social worker, once exclaimed that social work is "a crazy profession. They pay you to do what society doesn't want to have to do—deal with the handicapped, old people, minorities—but you are supposed to solve the problems cheaply and invisibly, and do it only for 'love.' But to do it to meet your own needs means you are crazy too. And then you perpetuate the problem, they say. It's really a bind."

So social workers don't have it easy, either with respect to their work or with the achievement of social status. In order to build his or her own esteem for the self and the profession, every social worker needs to examine and recognize what the profession actually stands for and what it does, even in the worker's own particular setting. Is, for example, the profession's purpose of enhancing human functioning and alleviating human suffering being advanced at Urban Day? Is this a job that needs to be done? Does it make society a better place? Does it improve the lives of those it serves? What would happen if it were not done? In the context of Urban Day, the answer to this last question is that many children would be increasingly and permanently handicapped, at great personal cost to themselves and their families and later on to society in the form of expensive institutionalization. This is a life work to be proud of. Let other people know about it!

Mrs. Haley muses thoughtfully that in a way, society clearly does value our profession and what we do. Ironically, this occurs when a family "falls through the cracks of the system," as when a family is evicted from its apartment for lack of rent and lands out on the street. Then, a local radio or TV station may take up the family's cause, and private citizens will often contribute generously to help the family relocate. People really do have an altruistic desire for social justice and to protect the unfortunate. This is the sort of work they hire social workers to do, but in some cases the families do not know where to go for help until it is too late, or the agencies they turn to cannot help, at least financially, because the people do not meet the criteria for financial assistance from the public programs. If more people knew about and appreciated the accomplishments of individual social workers and hence the contributions of the social work profession as a whole, perhaps more societal resources would eventually be made available to further its work.

This discussion has admittedly focused upon protecting and enhancing the dignity and integrity of the profession rather than vigorously critiquing it. This bias is intentional. Social workers are probably already their own worst critics. They know, for example, that sometimes their efforts do foster dependence, and they know better than anyone else that their caseloads are so heavy they cannot give the best quality service to everyone. Sometimes professional knowledge, skills, and resources do not prove equal to an important task. In order to continue to develop better professional knowledge and skills, social workers should certainly critique the profession, identify its shortcomings, and work to improve its services. However, it is the contention of this book that the greater need at this time is for the profession's special perceptions and contributions to be more fully recognized and valued, especially by social workers themselves.

At Urban Day, Mrs. Haley has been instrumental in changing the view of one upper-level administrator regarding the potential of professional social work intervention. This has occurred gradually and over a long period of time. For example, because so many of Urban Day's parents neglect to send their children to the center initially, or get them there irregularly and unclean, Mrs. Ramleau felt very pessimistic about them at one time. She didn't think social work services could make a difference. She believed that nothing could done to change these families' behavior. And people who had potential to pull themselves up by their own bootstraps wouldn't have let themselves fall so low in the first place, she reasoned.

Mrs. Haley listened carefully to Mrs. Ramleau's thoughts and agreed with a good part of them. "Yes," she affirmed, "people do need to do things for themselves; the motivation does have to be there on the inside. But," she added from time to time, "sometimes it helps to listen attentively, to let people hear themselves talk, to begin to crystallize their thoughts for the first time and hear them reflected back by an interested human being."

Mrs. Haley pointed out that through listening, a dialogue can begin, and a social worker can start to elicit from, or suggest to the client new alternatives. Helping people solve problems takes creativity, she observed. Social work requires more skill, ability to analyze quickly, knowledge of resources, and flexibility than most other professions. It requires, in addition, incredible patience and persistence.

Through her personal experience at Urban Day, Mrs. Ramleau has observed many positive changes in families she initially believed were hopeless. She has seen chronically absent children begin to attend on a regular basis, children with irregular behavior patterns begin to stabilize. Not all of them to be sure, but a good number, as in the cases of Bobbie Johnston and Richard Jenkins.

Lately, Mrs. Ramleau observed to Mrs. Haley: "I've really changed over time regarding how I look at these families." She now perceives that many apparently hopeless cases are not, given skilled intervention. This is a good example of how one social worker in one agency has helped to protect and enhance the dignity and integrity of the social work profession to an administrative superior. Over time, she has been able to demonstrate the value of its perspectives and skills in terms of concrete results. But these results might not have been noted for what they were without Mrs. Haley's vigorous discussion of professional purposes and the skills required to achieve them.

Taking Action Against Unethical Conduct

The second provision of the code concerning maintaining the integrity of the profession is as follows: "The social worker should take action through appropriate channels against unethical conduct by any other member of the profession."

In Chapter 4, we introduced the case of Diana Kinsman and her child, Dorothy. At the time that chapter was written, Dorothy was still in foster care though her case had recently been in court again. Mrs. Haley and Diana had felt confident the child would be returned at that hearing, because all the criteria established for return of the child had been met by the mother. However, as the reader will recall, the social worker assigned to the case by Blue County Protective Services failed to present the evidence favorable to Diana in court, and so the child was left in foster care. Mrs. Haley was shocked by the worker's behavior in court and believed it was professionally unethical. The protective services worker also failed to honor the contract she had developed and signed in conjunction with the mother, Mrs. Haley, and the attorneys. Professional courtesy alone should have dictated notifying Mrs. Haley prior to the court date of any intentions to change the agreement. To go to court and testify that the conditions required for the return of the child had not been met, when they indeed had been met and documented, was simply unethical. Moreover, on the human side, the decision involved a tremendous setback to Diana's slowly developing trust and sense of purpose.

This is the sort of case for which the second provision under the integrity maintainenance principle was written. It is conceivable that Mrs. Haley could have sat back after the court decision and allowed the mother to wait helplessly for her child until the next scheduled court appearance six months later. Had she done that, the mother might have lost the faith—partly in social workers and partly in herself—that was motivating her toward positive change. She had made many positive changes in her parenting practices, only to have them ignored by the protective services worker and the court.

So Mrs. Haley let the protective services worker know in strong terms that she felt the worker's actions were unethical, and that she intended to take the case back to court on appeal as soon as possible. Once more, however, Mrs. Haley attempted to avoid the adversarial perspective. If Mrs. Haley had gotten enmeshed in the normal win–lose perspective of the court, she might simply have scheduled an appeal date and waited until then to let the court determine the outcome. Winning the case that way might have been dramatic and emotionally gratifying. It would also have taken quite a bit of extra time and would have entailed greater risk. What Mrs. Haley did instead was first to have Diana Kinsman's attorney schedule the next possible court appeal date in case the outcome had to be determined that way. Then she called everyone involved back to a problem-solving meeting at Urban Day. She gathered her documentation carefully for that meeting, including records from Dorothy's teacher at Urban Day and the mother's psychologist, to demonstrate evidence of Diana's growing capacity for and skills in parenting. In this way, Mrs. Haley was able to convince the protective services worker that if the case went back to court, there would be a powerful case presented to support Diana's readiness for parenthood. She also listened to the concerns of the worker and her attorneys, and agreed to make certain new provisions in the parenting contract with Diana. The worker and the protective services attorneys then settled out of court, and little Dorothy came home. Dorothy and Diana still spend a good deal of time at Urban Day where they benefit from the teaching, therapy, and support the agency and its staff provides.

While the major purpose of the code of ethics is to provide social workers with a carefully developed set of guidelines for ethical practice, given the assumption that most social workers would want to practice ethically if they only knew how, it should be pointed out here that unethical practice may be punishable even where it is unintentional. The preamble of the code begins: "This code is intended to serve as a guide to the everyday conduct of members of the social work profession and as a basis for adjudication of issues in ethics when the conduct of social workers is alleged to deviate from the standards expressed or implied in this code."

Members of the National Association of Social Workers may ask to have cases of alleged unethical conduct by their peers reviewed by a special body of the NASW itself. In addition, social work is a licensed profession in certain states. Licensing is an important step forward for social workers, because the procedure establishes important educational and practice criteria regarding who may legally call him- or herself a social worker, and in this way protects clients from unprofessional service. But a licensed social worker can be tried in court for practice which violates the standards of the licensing body.

Even in a state where licensing laws do not exist, and in a circumstance where the NASW or the NASW code of ethics is not specifically involved, a social worker may be tried in court for conduct violating legal obligations. For example, in the state where Urban Day is located, two social workers were tried and convicted for contempt of court. They had been ordered by the court to report immediately should a certain teenager fail to comply with a court-ordered foster-care arrangement and a drug treatment program. The teenager ran away from the assigned group home and never reported for the drug treatment program. The workers failed to make the required report to the court. They were convicted and fined for contempt.

It is important for social workers to recognize that legal obligations are increasingly a part of the social work profession. Good intentions notwithstanding, failure to honor a court requirement can lead to legal prosecution. In the above-mentioned case, the court report notes specifically that heavy caseloads and overwork may have led to unintentional neglect of the court-ordered obligations. Nonetheless, it was the verdict of the court that overwork and lack of intentional neglect were not acceptable excuses for failure to honor legal obligations.

At first glance, convicting overburdened social workers for contempt of court seems unconscionable. But in time, such court orders, albeit over the probably undeserving bodies of the first victims, may lead to better practice conditions. After all, if social workers know they can be convicted of contempt of court for not carrying out court orders involving clients, and if they also recognize that the size of required caseloads makes it impossible to carry out all court orders, they may simply begin to refuse to carry these unreasonable loads. They will recognize it is too dangerous for them personally and professionally. And then, since the need will still be there, the funds may finally be allocated to hire sufficient numbers of qualified social workers. This is pipedream in a sense. But society really does want people to supervise delinquents, negotiate foster care, provide homes for the senile aged, and perform a number of other social control functions. It does not really want all that trouble out there unsupervised on the street. It just wants, as Mrs. Haley remarked so clearly, to have someone do it all "cheaply and invisibly." And social workers, the sorts of people who respond to need, have probably tried too long to stretch themselves beyond their limits to meet these needs because not enough qualified people were hired to do it properly. On the pessimistic side, of course, society may alternatively continue to choose to build more and bigger jails, as it has been doing for the past few years. It should be noted at this point that that which is legal may not always be that which is clearly most ethical. Our social justice system is not always just. Social workers sometimes must choose the best from a list of bad choices.

Provisions three and four concerning the integrity of the profession are relatively self-explanatory. Provision three states that "the social worker should act to prevent the unauthorized and unqualified practice of social work," and provision four that "the social worker should make no misrepresentation as to qualification, competence, service, or results to be achieved." In states with licensing laws for social workers, prevention of unqualified social work practice is much easier. However, even these laws may not be terribly effective because (1) most social work positions except private practice are not covered, and (2) money is not available to licensure boards to hire staff necessary to investigate complaints. But in many states, including the one where Urban Day is located, anyone can call him- or herself a social worker. And in the name of saving money, social service agencies may hire totally inexperienced and untrained people to handle the work, to the detriment of clients.

It will be recalled that even Urban Day hires nondegreed people as community workers in the social service department. Mrs. Haley hired her staff at a time when recruiting from among the "grass roots" was acceptable and even encouraged for entry-level social work positions. In order to assure competent practice among her community workers, she provides ongoing training in social work values, skills, and ethics. Her current staff does excellent work now due to their years of experience, but Mrs. Haley plans to hire staff with accredited degrees in social work when her current workers choose to leave. From her experience in working with social work student interns, Mrs. Haley has found that they bring with them to Urban Day a high level of knowledge and skill and a holistic outlook that enables them to develop into effective workers at the center very quickly.

COMMUNITY SERVICE

The next principle of the code of ethics states: "Community Service—The social worker should assist the profession in making social services available to the general public."

The major professional organization for social workers, the National Assoication of Social Workers, maintains an active legislative branch which alerts members about important pending legislation. Members are urged to write, call, or visit their legislators or senators to express support for bills intended to provide new social services for the public. The NASW thus educates its own members concerning important social legislation, but it also needs its members to generate support for these bills. Writing letters and making phone calls to legislators regarding relevant bills is one way social work practitioners can "assist the profession in making social services available to the general public." They can also serve as expert witnesses before various congressional committees and subcommittees.

Provision two under this principle adds: "The social worker should support the formulation, development, enactment, and implementation of social policies of concern to the profession." One way to do this is to help provide the data that may be required to formulate a bill. For example, Mrs. Haley is now assisting a private group to gather evidence regarding the impact of recent budget cuts on families and children at Urban Day. In particular, she is gathering information on the relationship between the provision of day-care services and the incidence of abuse in welfare families, this in an effort to suggest what needs to be done now to reduce child abuse. This is a first step in formulating more effective social legislation. Social workers can undertake needs assessment studies such as this one themselves, or organize task forces to assist. They may then lobby to educate local authorities and state legislators concerning identified needs.

With respect to community service the code also states: "The social worker should contribute time and professional expertise to activities that promote respect for the utility, the integrity, and the competence of the social work profession." Mrs. Haley does this in many small ways at Urban Day. For example, she often serves as a guide when groups tour the agency. She regards this as an opportunity to do public relations work for the profession. She discusses the social service aspects of Urban Day as a specific example of what the profession has to offer. In this fashion, Mrs. Haley delivers her message to groups of middle-class parents, visitors from United Way and other funding sources, and school groups, among others. She explains that social services can help multiproblem families, but they can also be useful for middle-class clients as well. She explains, for example, how difficult it can be for parents to deal with their ambivalent feelings toward a handicapped child, regardless of social class background, and how helping parents resolve these feelings can make a fundamental difference in their lives. She illustrates how social work helps people learn that they *matter*, that their lives matter. Parents can then use the energy formerly invested in feeling afraid or guilty in dealing with their children instead. Mrs. Haley does this sort of public relations work for social work services with *every* tour group, and in this way also helps to clarify and support the purpose of Urban Day as an agency.

Another way Mrs. Haley recently has contributed to promoting the social work profession is by helping to develop a training tape on advocacy for minorities with developmental disabilities. While working with the voluntary group primarily responsible for the tape, she was able to ensure that the tape included information on the role of social work services in advocating for minorities.

Mrs. Haley also does public relations work on behalf of the social work perspective, or approach to analyzing and solving problems, with Urban Day staff itself. For example, the teaching staff was recently horrified when a child was sent to Urban Day clad only in a grocery bag. Their first reaction was to call the parent to complain. However, Mrs. Haley came upon the situation before the call was made. "The other day," she noted to the teachers, "remember how you asked a mother why she'd kept her child home for three days? When the mother told you it was because she had no clean clothes, you asked her to send the child in anyhow—remember? I'm really glad this family has sent the child in. Maybe the grocery bag is all they have right now—let's wait awhile before we say anything so as not to embarrass them. If they don't have any clean diapers, their only other choice may be to keep the child home."

The next day, the child wore an adult's underwear to school, and the following day no clothing at all. Since the bus seat got wet this way, something had to be done! Mrs. Haley again persuaded the teachers that a phone call to complain might not be the best way to approach the situation. There were positive aspects to the case from the social work point of view; the child was attending school regularly. Mrs. Haley offered to visit the family at their home, to see if she could find out quietly and privately why the child wasn't wearing diapers and what could be done about it.

Mrs. Haley brought a supply of diapers with her on her home visit but left them in her car when she went in to meet the parents. She did not want to jump to conclusions, but to assess the situation. Certainly on the face of things it looked as if this family was currently too poor to purchase its own diapers, but then again, that might not be the case. Mrs. Haley had known families who sent their children to school in dirty diapers hoping to get the free supply of clean ones they got that way the month before. Mrs. Haley had to confront families like that, to avoid furthering dependency.

This was the first incident of this sort in connection with this family, however, and as Mrs. Haley suspected, dependency was not the problem. Poverty was. When she reached the child's home, both parents were present. As was her custom, she began the interview with small pleasantries. She was careful to praise this child's regular attendance at Urban Day. Eventually the atmosphere became sufficiently relaxed to introduce the topic of diapers. The father reflected sadly that he had been unable to take his baby to church on Father's Day because they hadn't been able to afford clean diapers. He was temporarily out of a job. So Mrs. Haley let the parents know she'd brought a supply with her if they'd like to have them. The father accepted with many words of thanks. He said then that he and his wife hadn't been sure what they should do about sending the child to Urban Day when they were out of these necessary items of clothing. Would it be preferable to keep the child home? Mrs. Haley assured the parents it was better to send the little girl to school, but that they could call the agency for a new supply of diapers when they really needed them. Subsequently, this family occasionally requested additional supplies during particularly tight times. They did not, however, abuse the privilege.

This case helps illustrate how the social work approach to problem solving allows service-as-usual to go on at Urban Day. Mrs. Haley continues to educate the staff regarding the social work approach to problem formulation and problem solving so that they will permit her to intervene in cases like these, greatly enhancing the chances for successful resolution. Her efforts have increased the staff's respect for the social work profession and what it has to offer.

DEVELOPMENT OF KNOWLEDGE

The third and last principle concerning the social worker's responsibility to the profession is: "Development of Knowledge—The social worker should take responsibility for identifying, developing, and fully utilizing know-ledge for professional practice." The code goes on to state: "The social worker should base practice upon recognized knowledge relevant to social work." This provision suggests the importance of seeking the best possible education in social work, so that the practitioner is familiar with the major sources of social work knowledge such as social science theory (particularly from the academic disciplines of sociology, anthropology, psychology, political science, and economics), perspectives from biology (especially concepts of genetics and the evolution of species), social work practice methods, methods of research, and professionally supervised field instruc-tion.

The second provision states that "the social worker should critically examine and keep current with emerging knowledge relevant to social work." This requirement can be difficult to honor due to time constraints and frequent work overload. Social workers employed by agencies which permit time off for refresher courses are most fortunate, as are those where in-service training sessions are provided during regular work hours. If these opportunities do not yet exist at one's place of employment, the worker should be encouraged to help develop them. Another way to keep oneself current is to subscribe to and read journals of social work. Joining the National Association of Social Workers and keeping up with its regular journal and other publications, both national and local, is an excellent way to do this. Many specialties within social work also produce one or more journals and are published on a regular basis. Finally, one can attend annual professional conferences.

The third and last provision under the principle concerning develop-ment of knowledge states: "The social worker should contribute to the knowledge base of social work and share research knowledge and practice wisdom with colleagues." A tall order indeed! For Mrs. Haley, working on this book is a personal example of contributing to the knowledge base of the profession. She points out that contributing to the knowledge base is especially difficult because it takes time, and yet it is not part of the job description for which she was hired at Urban Day. The time she puts in on the book is her own and is contributed after regular working hours. In addition, Mrs. Haley contributes to the knowledge base by conducting and encouraging in-house research projects in connection with various practice decisions at Urban Day. For example, personal hygiene is an issue at Urban Day. Frequently, children are sent to the center who, objectively speaking, are dirty in body and clothing and don't smell very good. Is this a problem the agency should try to deal with? If so, how, and under what circumstances?

It may surprise the reader to think that Urban Day might question whether hygiene was a problem warranting agency attention. Many people assume that it would be so as a matter of course. But it must be remembered that many Urban Day clients are extremely poor and come from such poor backgrounds that they might not be able to afford washing facilities, soap, and the extra clothes that frequent washing would require. The value of cleanliness might be a low priority as well, and time may be very limited, so that time spent cleaning might truly be time taken from more important tasks, such as supervising infants and young toddlers. So perhaps it would be best for an agency like Urban Day to let the problem go without mentioning it at all to the parents. Yet teachers forced to work in small classrooms with several particularly aromatic bodies certainly find the problem irritating and distracting. In fact, at Urban Day the nurse worries about skin rashes and other reactions in both children and staff.

Given this, Mrs. Haley decided to conduct a study of other agencies to find out whether they viewed cleanliness as a problem, and if so, what they did about it. In return, she promised to let participating agencies know the results of her study. She also went to the literature to find out what is written about hygiene. At the time of her initial inquiry she had the assistance of a graduate social work student placed with her for field instruction. The results of the study are still being compiled as this chapter is being written, but what Mrs. Haley has learned so far has been instructive. For example, all agencies doing work similar to Urban Day's in Project City report problems with hygiene and do perceive hygiene as a problem. What they have actually done about it varies greatly, however, and few guidelines exist in the literature.

Mrs. Haley hopes to be able to add to the knowledge base some day with regard to the issue of hygiene. To date, no clear answers exist. In her own experience, Mrs. Haley has found that talking with some parents in a straightforward manner about hygiene can lead to measurable improvements. But with others, the direct approach does not work at all. With still others, Mrs. Haley attempts to work on the problem through indirect means, as in the case of the Grant family.

Mrs. Grant maintained markedly substandard practices of hygiene for herself and her six children. Mrs. Haley became involved in this case when Mrs. Grant's little daughter, Ingrid, a deaf-blind child, was placed at Urban Day. Mrs. Haley deliberately chose not to deal with the issue of hygiene while Ingrid was at Urban Day. Mrs. Haley felt that the mother's difficulties were already overwhelming. Her husband had divorced her and left her to cope with all six children on her own, her physical health was poor, and her deaf and blind daughter, Ingrid, required a great deal of time and special attention. Mrs. Haley feared that an additional demand from Urban Day involving a negative perception of her current performance would crush this mother. Mrs. Haley chose instead to try to build Mrs. Grant's self-esteem.

In choosing to strengthen Mrs. Grant's self-esteem rather than focusing on her standards of hygiene, Mrs. Haley was selecting an approach that certain social science theories can validate. For example, research demonstrates that positive reinforcement usually produces the best results in bringing about positive behavioral change. Mrs. Haley hoped that by offering genuine praise and positive reinforcement for the brave job this mother was doing with her children, Mrs. Grant's self-esteem would improve. Mrs. Haley hoped that, as a by-product, Mrs. Grant's self-care, including personal hygiene, would improve at some later date. That was not a predictable by-product, however.

Mrs. Grant's self-esteem did seem to improve, and she began to enroll in classes where she could learn tactile sign language in order to communicate with her daughter. She also began to work as a volunteer in the Red Cross Meals on Wheels Program. Her standards of hygiene for self, home, and children may have improved slightly, but certainly not measurably. Mrs. Haley could have criticized Mrs. Grant especially for working as a volunteer at the Red Cross, instead of staying home to clean. But then where would Mrs. Grant have been able to build her self-respect through contributing to others? Mrs. Haley decided that the volunteer work was more important than the issue of hygiene, and she gave Mrs. Grant further praise.

But then little Ingrid graduated from Urban Day at the age of three and went on to enroll in a public preschool program for handicapped children. Shortly, she came home with a note complaining about cleanliness and odor. There were a couple more notes, each gaining in intensity. In embarrassment and indignation, Mrs. Grant went on a tirade. She yanked little Ingrid right out of school and refused to send her back. She stormed down to Mrs. Haley's office at Urban Day and ranted and raved, "I just won't be treated like that," she shouted. "Who does that teacher think she is?"

Mrs. Haley could have criticized Mrs. Grant for the apparently irresponsible decision of taking her child out of the preschool program. Instead, she listened, and then endeavored to give positive reinforcement. "Yes," Mrs. Haley said to the mother, "Ingrid does need to be in school. I don't know if you made the right decision here, but I know you did what you thought was best." She finished hearing the mother out and comforted her, because she knew the mother felt terribly upset about what she had done. As an interim step, she found a home trainer from the Center for Blind Children to help Mrs. Grant work with Ingrid at home.

A short while later, Mrs. Haley went and talked with Ingrid's former teacher at the public school, asking her if hygiene was really so important it was worth having the little girl taken out of school. The teacher, a caring young woman, had never expected her notes would lead to the child's being withdrawn from school, and she agreed she would rather have Ingrid back, dirty or not. Mrs. Haley also spoke to the school principal, and he felt the same way. Each agreed to meet with the mother to talk with her personally, if Mrs. Haley could arrange a conference.

Mrs. Haley, through her painstaking work that had resulted in Mrs. Grant trusting her implicitly, and through her mediating role with the public school authorities, was able to arrange a meeting at Mrs. Grant's home. On the day of the meeting, Mrs. Haley could hardly recognize the house. Mrs. Grant had scoured it until it was spotless, and she herself was scrubbed clean and more attractively attired than Mrs. Haley had ever seen her. The meeting was a success and Ingrid went back to school. Mrs. Haley notes that while cleanliness in the Grant home has never been a focus of her own intervention, housekeeping standards have perceptively improved in the past two years, and so has the hygiene of the children. She believes this is the cumulative effect of a nonjudgmental approach and self-esteem building through positive reinforcement. Still, a giant step was taken during the run-in with the teacher, an incident that would have been a real catastrophe without the supportive intervention of Mrs. Haley. Is there a correct approach to problems like hygiene? How can one determine what interventive techniques to use with whom? When? Making these decisions is still very much an art, but social workers would like to develop them more into a science. Only as we start to share our own experience and research can we make it more nearly so. As Mrs. Haley's efforts illustrate, ordinary practitioners can contribute to the development of the social work knowledge base by initiating research projects relevant to their current work and by sharing both research findings and related practices wisdom with colleagues. They can, of course, also contribute by helping with someone else's research. Simply by answering questionnaires, for example, social workers can help others with data collection.

In conclusion, this chapter has examined and discussed the fifth major section of the social work code of ethics, the social worker's ethical responsibility to the social work profession. The major principles included in this category are maintaining the integrity of the profession, community service, and the development of knowledge.

REVIEW

This chapter deals with the social worker's ethical responsibility to the social work profession. To assist the student in review, the fifth section of the social work code of ethics is reproduced in full below.

THE SOCIAL WORKER'S ETHICAL RESPONSIBILITY TO THE SOCIAL WORK PROFESSION

M. Maintaining the Integrity of the Profession. The social worker should uphold and advance the values, ethics, knowledge, and mission of the profession.
1. The social worker should protect and enhance the dignity and integrity of the profession and should be responsible and

vigorous in discussion and criticism of the profession.

2. The social worker should take action through appropriate channels against unethical conduct by any other member of the profession.
3. The social worker should act to prevent the unauthorized and unqualified practice of social work.
4. The social worker should make no misrepresentation in advertising as to qualifications, competence, service, or results to be achieved.

N. Community Service. The social worker should assist the profession in making social services available to the general public.

1. The social worker should contribute time and professional expertise to activities that promote respect for the utility, the integrity, and the competence of the social work profession.
2. The social worker should support the formulation, development, enactment, and implementation of social policies of concern to the profession.

O. Development of Knowledge. The social worker should take responsibility for identifying, developing, and fully utilizing knowledge for professional practice.

1. The social worker should base practice upon recognized knowledge relevant to social work.
2. The social worker should critically examine and keep current with emerging knowledge relevant to social work.
3. The social worker should contribute to the knowledge base of social work and share research knowledge and practice wisdom with colleagues.

STUDY QUESTIONS

1 What are some creative ways in which individual students can "uphold and advance the values, ethics, knowledge, and mission" of the social work profession?

2 In your opinion, is social work a "controversial profession" as the author apparently believes? Why or why not?

3 How might court enforcement of legal responsibilities of social workers eventually lead to better conditions for professional practice?

4 How might licensing laws help social workers "prevent the unauthorized and unqualified practice of social work?"

5 In what ways is Mrs. Haley contributing to the knowledge base of the social work profession?

6 In what ways is Mrs. Haley helping the social work profession in its goal to make social services available to more of the general public?

7 What kinds of efforts can individual social workers make to keep current with expanding knowledge pertaining to their work?

7

The Social Worker's Ethical Responsibility to Society

"I feel very strongly about the question of personal worth," the man said. "What I do in my job is make routine decisions for the state regarding authorization of medical treatment for people covered by Medicaid. If I make a decision people don't like, they can appeal to somebody higher up. All I do is follow the rules; I'm just a functionary. But the idea of the state providing thousands of dollars in medical care, say, for some old lady who has never contributed one cent to the state in tax dollars—that goes against my grain. I think we need to look at the notion of who deserves what medical treatment so that we can save millions of dollars being wasted through these programs."

"Ah—aren't decisions like that a bit political? Like the notion of who is worth what? Couldn't that kind of decision change with every national administration?" I ventured.

"Political? Of course not. These are routine matters of policy. It's just that it's foolish to waste money on people who haven't ever paid taxes into the system to maintain these programs."

What, indeed, is the worth of an anonymous old lady who, by definition in this discussion, hasn't ever been employed, meaning that she has never made a salary from which taxes have been withheld? If she gets sick when she grows old, should society spend money on her for medical care? Is she worth that? Why or why not? What sexism issues could be involved here that the medicaid functionary was totally unaware of? For example, if this hypothetical old lady had managed a household, raised children, nurtured, and thus enabled a husband to withstand the pressures of the job market, as she was probably taught was her role as a woman, what real contribution to the national economy did she make? What might have happened to her husband's productivity had she quit her end of the bargain? Her children's potential productivity? How was her contribution to society hidden so that this medicaid worker was quite unconscious of it? Is it possible that the question of human worth is political indeed?

PROMOTING THE GENERAL WELFARE

The sixth and final section of the social work code of ethics is titled, "The Social Worker's Ethical Responsibility to Society." The code identifies one major principle under this heading: "Promoting the General Welfare— The social worker should promote the general welfare of society."

Before we examine the provisions included under this principle, consider the problems touched upon in the introductory anecdote to this chapter. Who is society? Whose general welfare is to be promoted? Clearly, the medicaid functionary believes that his own general welfare would be enhanced if nontaxpaying old ladies, or at least nontaxpayers, were omitted from those eligible for medicaid payments. Presumably, he believes this would lower his personal tax burden. Other members of society strongly wish to hire only white males as employees, or only heterosexuals, or wish to live only in neighborhoods that comprise individuals exactly like themselves. They feel this would enhance their general welfare. Some large ethnic groups may wish to eliminate entirely certain minorities, such as American Indians, Australian Aboriginees, German Jews, or Turkish-born Armenians. They believe this would enhance their own general welfare.

The point is that society itself can promote beliefs, practices, and policies that enhance the welfare of one group at the expense of another. Social workers need to choose carefully the particular society whose general welfare they choose to support, and how they support it. Sometimes such choices involve value conflict; for example, Cousin Harry may generally favor social policies promoting civil rights and fair housing for minorities, but become totally confused when Aunt Minnie wishes to admit only whites to her boarding house. Shouldn't Aunt Minnie have the right to choose her own tenants? Is there really a fair answer to this question as long as society itself plants the seeds of discrimination by teaching prejudice to each and every one of us? Yet how can the seeds of discrimination be destroyed without personal experience challenging the stereotypes? Still, negative stereotypes may actually be reinforced if one's personal experience is with people from the stereotyped group who have been injured and angered over a long period of time so that they feel impelled to punish someone for their suffering. But should Aunt Minnie be the one forced to suffer in atonement?

Where are the fair answers? There really aren't any. In the language of the Bible, the sins of the fathers (and mothers) really are visited upon the sons (and daughters and aunts). Yet the social work code of ethics offers some guidelines which can help practitioners address these complex issues. They identify those parts of society toward which social workers have special responsibility, and where their professional practice may be used to achieve greater social justice and a better standard of living for all.

Preventing Discrimination

The first provision in the code of ethics under promoting the general welfare states: "The social worker should act to prevent and eliminate discrimination against any person or group on the basis of race, color, sex, sexual orientation, age, religion, national origin, marital status, political belief, mental or physical handicap, or any other preference or personal characteristic, condition, or status." Thus the code includes as a major focus of its protection those persons often unfairly treated by society at large, and further declares as a special responsibility of the profession the prevention of discrimination against disadvantaged minority groups. It goes without saying that since many powerful people within the larger society explicitly desire to discriminate against these groups, the social worker may find him- or herself frequently in conflict with the status quo and those persons who wish to maintain it.

Sex and color are probably the characteristics most likely to lead to discrimination in the United States today. The student will recall the case of Antonia described in Chapter 3. In this situation a little girl of minority ethnic heritage was ignored by a qualified physical therapist assigned to her public school special-education program, despite her obvious need for service. This was probably due to that therapist's attitudes toward poor people of color and possibly females. At Urban Day, daily efforts are exerted by the social workers to make sure that their clients are treated fairly despite their various handicapping conditions. The reader will recall how much effort was invested in securing for little Antonia her physical therapy, even after the case had been formally closed by Urban Day.

However, as Mrs. Haley carefully points out, discrimination goes on even at Urban Day in such subtle ways that it normally isn't even noticed. We are often blind to our own daily discriminatory practices. For example, Urban Day as an agency doesn't expect much of parents. In truth, most parents make few demands on the agency because they feel powerless in society as a whole, and are likewise afraid to assert themselves at Urban Day. Most are conspicuous by their absence. But Urban Day subtly encourages the absence of parents by myriad virtually unnoticed practices. First of all, parents have to accept Urban Day's entire program in order for their children to receive any service at all. This practice discriminates against the parents in that it strongly diminishes their power to interact with and direct the development of their children while they are in the agency setting. As a result, the agency's manifest and admirable policy of aiding chilidren masks subtle devaluation of the parents.

As another example of the same sort of thing, most of the work with the children is performed one-on-one. This practice is so common in agencies like Urban Day that it goes almost unquestioned. Besides, that is how this service is billed to and paid for by medicaid (*x* dollars per unit of service to a particular child), which helps freeze the practice as it is.

But Mrs. Haley observes that if the agency viewed parents as intricately involved with the development of their children, as they are in fact, the bulk of the agency's efforts would then be directed toward training the parents to work with their own children. This could be done in the supportive and educational environment of the agency, in small groups in the therapy rooms or in the classrooms including the teacher, as well as in the home setting. In this way the skills required for appropriately stimulating the children could be shared by teachers and therapists with parents. They could then be invested in the children far more frequently and consistently, with therapists, teachers, and parents working together as a skilled team. If such participatory efforts from parents were expected and such training offered as part and parcel of Urban Day's program, Mrs. Haley believes that most parents would respond. Not only the children but the parents would benefit from their new skills and ability to contribute. But again, expected practice at Urban Day is treatment given by the therapist to the child, and the expected mode of payment is per unit of service to a given child. With these blinders, no other possible approach to service is even imagined except by the creative few, who are often viewed as idealistic and impractical.

In coming to terms with the concept of discrimination, then, it is important to look beyond the surface of things. Practices which are normal and ordinary in a given setting may hide some very real discrimination that nobody notices. If the people who are thus discriminated against perceive themseleves as powerless, they will probably not bring the practice to anybody's attention. Or, they may not even notice the discrimination for what it is, viewing their reality simply as the way things are. Is that OK then, if nobody seems to mind? Since Urban Day's clients don't complain, is it OK to leave things just as they are? Mrs. Haley thinks not, and has been trying to educate the staff regarding the need to work seriously with parents for a long time. But sometimes many other circumstances need to change as well for a different perspective to be adopted. Mrs. Haley's hunch is that it will take some major changes external to the agency, such as new government funding criteria, or a major social upheaval encouraging minority clients to demand more involvement with and accountability to themselves by the agency, to bring about any fundamental change.

Ensuring Access to Resources

The next provision of the code concerning the social worker's responsibility to society states: "The social worker should act to ensure that all persons have access to the resources, services, and opportunities which they require." What an enormous directive in so few words! Persons everywhere have need for more resources than they have—money, food, clothing, housing, love, acceptance, education, employment, and so on ad infinitum. Human need is so great in fact that if any given social worker took it upon him- or herself to "ensure that all persons have access to the resources, services, and opportunities which they require," that worker would probably collapse in panic or burned-out apathy. Nonetheless, this provision of the code is meant to be taken very seriously. And equally obviously, in order to survive personally and professionally, each social worker must carefully consider how to apply it to him- or herself in particular.

To begin with, the "all persons" who must be ensured access to resources referred to in this provision of the code probably is not intended literally to include all persons in the world who have needs. That responsibility would be too overwhelming for anyone. More likely the provision is intended to emphasize that the social worker should serve all persons who come to him or her in need, regardless of their personal characteristics, condition, or status. Even more, it implicitly guides the social worker toward social action. Should existing agency or social policy discriminate against or otherwise fail to meet the needs of a given group who come to the worker for assistance, the social worker should exert efforts to change those policies so that these needs can be met (as explicitly stated in provision six under this principle of the code). This obligation is in accordance with the generalist model of social work practice, in which the social worker is expected to problem-solve in whatever systems are required in each particular situation.

However, any given social worker cannot meet all needs of all people. Practically speaking, within the clear guideline that a worker may not discriminate against clients on the basis of race, color, sex, etc., the worker must still exercise choice regarding the types of needs he or she will address in practice. This need to select, to focus one's efforts, is not explicit in the code, but must be viewed as the most reasonable interpretation.

Our selection of the social problems or clients we will work with begins with the type of agency or private practice we select for employment. If we choose an agency whose major purpose is community organization, development, and social action, then we will spend most of our working hours helping very large groups of people gain new access to resources. We can even reach out beyond the "helping all people who come to us" model and assist people who haven't come to us, thus adopting a preventive model of social work intervention. However, our choice of agency will still limit and direct our energies, so that we channel them in behalf of a particular group of people, such as migrant farm workers, the unemployed, older people, or women.

The work we do for our agency will normally involve at least eight hours of our day. We may choose to work with other social problems as well, perhaps on a volunteer basis, and thus help alleviate injustices other than those addressed at our primary agency of employment. But our focus must still be limited due to the fact that there are only twenty-four hours in a day. And personal, self-care needs must be recognized and honored as part of the whole configuration of life goals. In addition to work, we need, at the very least, friends, family, food, and play just to keep going. All these require quality and quantity investments of time. Then there is sleep! We cannot singlehandedly do everything that is desperately needed in the world right now. But on the other hand, perhaps collectively as a profession we can make an impact on human need.

At Urban Day, Mrs. Haley has sometimes been in a quandary as to just where to exert her efforts on behalf of the clients of her own agency. Urban Day, it must be admitted, is primarily a casework-oriented agency in that the needs of the individual children and families are worked with one by one. This makes it more difficult to use Urban Day's experiences to illustrate the ethical responsibilities of the social work practitioner to society than it would be if Urban Day were a "social action" type of agency. On the other hand, Urban Day itself, as an agency, is the product of social action. The founders of Urban Day, it will be recalled, were social workers who were ethically motivated to promote the general welfare of society by meeting the needs of handicapped, mostly poor and minority children living in Project City. The creation of Urban Day was their means of ensuring access to resources for people who previously wouldn't have had any hope of receiving them.

Despite the fact that Urban Day is primarily a casework-oriented agency, and as the generalist model of social work practice would both predict and reflect, there are many circumstances in which Mrs. Haley must devote some of her professional efforts to societal issues. For example, as the national government changed its food stamp policy in a way that cut down availability of food to many of Urban Day's clients, Mrs. Haley was confronted with a large number of hungry people who needed new sources of food. Should Mrs. Haley exert her time and energy to develop a food bank at Urban Day? Or to advocate to change federal food stamp policy? But how could she do either of these things seriously and still perform her regular job at the agency, coordinating admissions, chasing down absent children, taking people to appointments, supervising students and staff, counseling discouraged parents, serving on multidisciplinary teams, making knowledgeable referrals, and advocating staff needs with upper-level administrators? All these things needed to be done with care, but for how long could one person attempt them all without burning out entirely? Mrs. Haley makes these types of decisions day to day, choosing among the most pressing needs of the moment after weighing them against her professional goals, including her own need to remain sane.

Mrs. Haley decided that trying to develop a large food bank at Urban Day would require an immense amount of organizational effort that would be too time consuming. So she chose, instead, to learn where existing food banks were located in the city and referred needy clients to them. Some supplies were collected at Urban Day to handle emergencies when the food banks themselves stood empty. Once Mrs. Haley made the staff aware of the need, many joined the effort to keep Urban Day's emergency food shelves filled. For example, Bonnie Nichols brought the need at Urban Day to the attention of her church, and the church began to donate regularly. Mrs. Ramleau located some large sources of inexpensive food, and Theodore Tell allocated certain moneys from the agency's general funds for the purchase of food.

Mrs. Haley also wrote to appropriate legislators regarding food stamp policies and the changes she perceived to be necessary. She feels that this approach to "solving" the food problem is the best she can do under today's circumstances, but knows it is not enough. All too often the food banks in Project City do stand empty in these difficult times. Yet one person can only do so much.

On a more everyday scale, Mrs. Haley reports that she finds herself doing little things all the time to ensure access to resources for her clients, particularly at Urban Day itself. For example, a deaf couple recently brought their child in for evaluation, and these parents wanted to be part of the evaluation process. That would require the employment of an interpreter for the deaf, which they could not afford. Urban Day did not have such an interpreter available. So Mrs. Haley sought and gained the administration's approval to employ an interpreter for the evaluation.

Mrs. Haley wished to make the agency parents' group available to this deaf couple as well. That would involve a continual need for an interpreter. This request was denied by the administration, which pleaded it couldn't afford to provide such a service on a regular basis. So Mrs. Haley is currently contacting schools and other potential sources of skilled volunteers. Her purpose is to avoid discrimination against physically handicapped parents, believing they should have access to all the resources of the agency available to other parents.

As this section has been discussing, the social work code of ethics requires practitioners to "ensure that all persons have access to the resources, services, and opportunities that they require." This requirement, as noted above, creates a real issue for the worker in terms of the need to balance personal requirements with professional responsibilities. In order to avoid burnout, the practitioner must develop a life-style which provides him- or herself with nurturance and energy resources, and these personal requirements take *time*. Special time designed for personal renewal takes time away from professional responsibilities. How can the two needs be balanced? Each practitioner will have to answer this question according to his or her unique needs and interests.

As a general guideline, it may be suggested that personal time taken in self-care can be viewed as a responsible professional investment as well. A depleted self cannot function well, personally *or* professionally. Each worker must, therefore, select issues and concerns of particular interest to deal with on a regular basis; work that responds to personal interests can generate as well as deplete one's personal energy. One can also exercise certain important rights and responsibilities of citizenship, such as voting and participating in selected demonstrations, without investing an inordinate amount of time. But may worthy causes will need to be left to someone else. The profession as a whole must move to ensure that all people gain access to the resources they need; each practitioner can take action to meet just a part of the need.

Expanding Choice and Opportunity

The code also provides that "the social worker should act to expand choice and opportunity for all persons, with special regard for disadvantaged or oppressed groups and persons." In the case in which Mrs. Haley sought to make agency resources accessible to deaf as well as hearing parents, she is also "helping expand choice and opportunity for all persons." Mrs. Haley points out, however, that she wants attendance at parents' meetings to be a choice for the deaf parents, and not to be more of an obligation for them than it is for other parents. Thus the interpreter will need to understand that the parents might or might not attend all the meetings. It may, therefore, be necessary to devise a system whereby the deaf parents can let the interpreter know when she or he will be needed.

In addition, the entire social service staff of Urban Day is continually involved in trying to expand clients' choices and opportunities. Card files describing community resources to help make appropriate referrals are continually revised and kept up-to-date by the social service staff. Mrs. Dillon is the specialist in this area. Parents are urged to undertake further education and job training wherever possible, so that they may have a chance to develop their employability and reduce their dependency on public income maintenance programs.

Sometimes the opportunity to expand choice arrives in unexpected forms. For example, in the case of the Grant family described in the last chapter, opportunity arrived in the form of the Red Cross. As the reader will recall, Mrs. Grant became involved in working with the Red Cross Meals on Wheels program. She really didn't have enough spare time to get involved in such volunteer work, given her six children including one deaf and blind daughter, and the fact that she really should have been investing her time cleaning her home and children according to the normal priorities of society. But far from discouraging Mrs. Grant from her volunteer work, Mrs. Haley encouraged it, knowing the energy she invested would be returned in many ways, beginning with increased self-esteem. The contact with the Red Cross yielded many rewards, ranging from self-esteem to such practical benefits as the chance to take home food leftovers. More recently, the volunteer work has given the family access to ample supplies of used clothing as well. Given the large size of her family, these additional material goods have been of great assistance to the struggling mother.

Mrs. Grant now also assists her Meals on Wheels office in coordinating its volunteer program. She is considering training in social work once her children are old enough to be on their own. To be sure, Mrs. Grant is just one parent on Mrs. Haley's caseload, and not every deserving single mother is so fortunate or so motivated. However, little successes like this one provide energy and spirit to the social worker as well as to the client, and can help the good work go on.

Respect for Diversity

Little Herbie Goldstein was referred to Urban Day because he had the misfortune to be born with Down's syndrome. Herbie was also born Jewish, the first child of a professional, upwardly mobile middle-class couple. Herbie's parents were shattered by their son's handicap. Many parents feel that their lives are shattered by the birth of a Down's syndrome baby. For a Jewish couple the experience of tragedy may be especially strong, however, because intellectual acumen is so highly prized in the Jewish culture. This is especially true for eldest sons.

Herbie was a cute little boy and since the staff was very used to a variety of handicapped children, they soon came to view him as one of their most adorable, attractive, and capable children, with the potential to learn to care for himself. He was sweet to the staff and quick to learn by the standards of the agency. But because of the staff's understandable attachment to Herbie, it was impossible for them to accept Herbie's parents at first. The parents clearly viewed this lovely little boy as a source of total despair and dejection, as the ruination of their lives. Much as they may have wanted to love Herbie, they couldn't, and their rejection was obvious. They didn't want to cuddle him or talk to him, or even be around him very much when they visited the agency. The staff felt protective of the little boy and angry at the parents for their coldness.

To make matters worse, the parents didn't improve their standing with the staff by insisting on special formula, cereals, eating utensils, dishes, and the like for their son, as they kept Kosher. Further, in keeping with their religious tradition, they kept their son at home on certain days. The staff soon lost patience with the parents and viewed them as difficult and picky. The family didn't fit Urban Day's usual casual style. These were parents who made demands on the agency and expected their demands to be met, rare indeed in this setting, and yet they were not particularly involved with or appreciative of those parts of Herbie's care that the staff felt were very important, such as his educational and physical therapy programs.

How does one cope with parents who made many demands on the staff about things the staff considered unimportant, like special meals and utensils, and yet who didn't seem very interested in the quality of the attention and therapy the staff poured into the boy? In an effort to better understand the parents' perspectives and values, Mrs. Haley hastily researched Jewish cultural traditions. She began with some agency staff members who were Jewish, although from a more liberal tradition. In addition, she did some reading on Judaism. What she learned was that intellectual excellence was extremely important to traditional Jews. More than being just a value, its presence had made the difference between surviving and perishing as a people throughout history in a frequently hostile world.

Little Herbie, however, would never be able to meet the expected standard for intelligence of his culture or his family, regardless of the amount of skilled teaching and therapy he received. Not ever, no matter what. And his parents knew that. No wonder they were especially upset, seemed uninterested in Herbie's educational programming, and focused on things that they could make right: the proper elements of the Kosher tradition. Perhaps later on, as they came to know the little boy as a person, they might be able to care more for him as an individual with special needs. Another strong Jewish value, after all, is the protection of children and other vulnerable persons.

Meanwhile, the staff would have to cope, and so would the parents. Mrs. Haley worked to reframe the parents' behavior for the staff: "Many families don't accept handicapped children at first," and "We all have our cultural traditions that are important to us, like Christmas trees at Christmas, and so we need to respect those of others." In this way she was able to present the family in a way that was more acceptable to staff, and the parents were more sensitively treated at Urban Day as a result. Her work to help the family accept little Herbie, on the other hand, is really just beginning. At this point the parents cannot consciously admit to themselves that they don't accept their son. But work to help people cope with their own reality is part of day-to-day social work practice. The fact that social workers work with people from diverse cultural and life-style traditions makes the work more complicated, but also more stimulating, thought-provoking, and growth-producing than it would be if everyone were alike.

Not only other agency staff but also social workers themselves may have trouble dealing with diversity and accepting differences among people. For example, one worker may feel comfortable working with members of diverse cultural groups but be quite uncomfortable working with clients of the opposite sex. A different worker might feel quite comfortable working with clients of the opposite sex but be uncomfortable dealing with people who are physically disabled. Workers must allow themselves to feel, to consciously experience their own biases so that they can recognize them. Once biases are recognized, practitioners will be better able to make the effort necessary to exhibit ethical behavior towards these clients, their feelings of discomfort notwithstanding. In certain circumstances, workers may, however, legitimately choose to transfer clients to other workers whose feelings will be less likely to interfere with responsible service.

Public Emergencies

The next provision of the code deals with social work professional responsibility in public emergencies: "The social worker should provide appropriate professional services in public emergencies." Since there hasn't been a public emergency in Project City, where Urban Day is located, the experience of this agency's social service staff cannot help illustrate this provision of the code. But the code is here for social workers who find themselves caught up in such disasters as major storms, floods, or nuclear holocaust, urging them to use their skills to help others survive, and hopefully to reestablish their lives.

Shaping Social Policy

The final two provisions of the code of ethics concern social policy. Provision six states: "The social worker should advocate changes in policy and legislation to improve social conditions and to promote social justice," and provision seven states, "The social worker should encourage informed participation by the public in shaping social policies and institutions."

Mrs. Haley works at these things on a regular basis. Though her job at Urban Day makes it impossible for her to work toward social change full time (as a social worker employed for a community organization type of agency might be able to do), she nevertheless considers it her responsibility to express her professional opinions, share her practice knowledge, and chip away at nonproductive public policy as much as she can. For example, she frequently writes letters to legislators and others to express her position on causes of importance. She has, for example, written letters about problems with medicaid funding, Aid to Families with Dependent Children, food stamps, cuts in school lunch programs, child abuse legislation, and the like. She has participated on local professional committees to help maintain quality social work service in times of severe budget cuts. She has worked with the NASW in support of licensure. She has served on boards of directors to help influence the policy developments of such programs as Foster Grandparents and Women's Crisis Line. She has attended many public hearings, in particular those reviewing proposed revisions in the public law providing services to handicapped children.

In addition, Mrs. Haley encourages "informed participation of the public" in shaping social policy. She encourages professional colleagues and especially clients to express themselves verbally, write letters, and attend hearings on matters of importance to promoting the general welfare. Mrs. Haley says she believes in encouraging clients, staff, friends, and neighbors to speak out, tell what they know, validate the fact that changes are needed. It is important to fight the idea that "nothing I do makes a difference," she exclaims fervently. She feels that efforts toward positive change must be continuous, and that continuous efforts can indeed make a difference. Whenever a client or a staff member at Urban Day sinks into hopeless complaining about a perceived injustice, she encourages that person to think about what he or she can do about it. Whom can the aggrieved person call? Write? Speak to in person? She recalls a client who was denied SSI (Supplemental Security Income, in this case for a permanent physical disability) due to a minor technicality. The need for financial and medical assistance was real, and the technicality, while small, would present an unreasonable hardship to correct. So Mrs. Haley suggested the client write the governor of the state to describe her plight. She did, with a supportive letter from Mrs. Haley, and the governor granted her the SSI on appeal. The resolution of her case, of course, set a precedent for someone else in the same situation.

Not all things are possible. Yet if educated effort is exerted in a considered way, more things may be possible than anyone ever expected. At the stage of our history during which this book is being written, the simple act of voting, if undertaken by a majority of social service clients, could make a tremendous difference in national public policy. So Mrs. Haley, along with many other social workers, also strongly encourages her clients and colleagues to vote.

In conclusion, this chapter has examined the sixth and last section of the social work code of ethics, the social worker's ethical responsibility to society. The code identifies one major principle under this heading: promoting the general welfare. We have seen how the task of social workers includes influencing the decision making that determines whether resources are available, and to whom. These decisions are made at many levels, by many institutions including national, state, and local governments as well as social service agencies. Working for more resources for particular clients, as well as for social justice for all, takes considerable effort and time. Social workers must learn how to balance these activities with the demands of their jobs, and with their own personal needs as individuals, family members, and friends.

REVIEW

The final section of the code of ethics deals with the social worker's ethical responsibility to society. Social workers will need to meet this responsibility in creative and individual ways, depending upon their personal interests, talents, and needs, and their agency of employment. The following is the complete text of this heading of the code, as adopted by the National Association of Social Workers in 1979.

THE SOCIAL WORKER'S ETHICAL RESPONSIBILITY TO SOCIETY

P.   Promoting the General Welfare. The social worker should promote the general welfare of society.
1.   The social worker should act to prevent and eliminate discrimination against any person or group on the basis of race, color, sex, sexual orientation, age, religion, national origin, marital status, political belief, mental or physicl handicap, or any other preference or personal characteristic, condition, or status.
2.   The social worker should act to ensure that all persons have access to the resources, services, and opportunities which they require.
3.   The social worker should act to expand choice and opportunity for all persons, with special regard for disadvantaged or oppressed groups and persons.
4.   The social worker should promote conditions that encourage respect for the diversity of cultures which constitute American society.
5.   The social worker should provide appropriate professional services in public emergencies.
6.   The social worker should advocate changes in policy and legislation to improve social conditions and to promote social justice.
7.   The social worker should encourage informed participation by the public in shaping social policies and institutions.

STUDY QUESTIONS

1   How much do you think the anonymous old lady referred to in the introductory section of this chapter is "worth?" What do you want to know in order to answer this question? How does the question, and what you want to know before you can answer it, help to reveal your own particular values?

2 Define "society." What does the author mean by writing that "society itself can promote beliefs, practices and policies that enhance the immediate general welfare of one group at the expense of another?"

3 What does the author mean by stating that "the sins of the fathers (and mothers) really are visited on the sons (and daughters and aunts)"? Do you think she is right? Why or why not?

4 What are examples of discrimination that Mrs. Haley perceives at Urban Day? Many of the other staff at Urban Day may not perceive these practices as examples of discrimination. What do you think? Why?

5 According to this chapter, what important personal and professional factors do social workers need to consider while working to meet the ethical principle of promoting the general welfare?

6 How is Urban Day itself an example of what can be achieved when social workers work to promote the general welfare?

7 Define self-care. What practices and considerations are important in attending to self-care? How might these differ from person to person, agency setting to agency setting?

Epilogue

M. KATHLEEN MASCH

I feel a certain amount of anxiety and humility in being a part of writing this book. I knew from the outset of this project that this book would not, and could not, definitively illustrate the social work code of ethics. That is a process that is our responsibility, individually, as social workers. Each of you who read this book, as you live and practice social work, will illustrate the code of ethics in your own way. You will be part of the creative process of defining the code of ethics as a framework for practice just as lawyers define the meanings of laws as they impact on people's lives in the changing context of society.

I remember my life as a student and as a young practitioner and my need to find a framework for all of the knowledge and theories that I was to use to help others. For me, the code of ethics provided this framework. If an idea, a theory, or a mode of practice did not fit within this framework then it needed to be reexamined, modified, or discarded. My hope is that this book will help you see how the code of ethics can be used as a tool that will help you define and develop your practice.

My anxiety relates to the fact that you may judge Urban Day too harshly. I have come to love this agency as a living, growing thing, and participating in the writing of this book has been a very enlightening process. If, as you read the examples, you find instances where we have violated one part of the code while looking at another, remember, we're human and made the best decisions we could at the time. We grow and change from these decisions as you will in your practice. Remember that social work practice is a process and as we gain more experience and information we can improve on that process and become better practitioners.

My humility comes from reading this book as a finished product and realizing how little is said about our administrators, teachers, therapists aides, and nurse. This is not a book about early childhood intervention so the work done by others in that area at Urban Day is not highlighted in the way it deserves. I feel humbled by the knowledge that I am a small part of the caring and concern for parents and children at Urban Day. All the other staff besides social workers are also confronted with practice decisions on a daily basis. I think it is our responsibility as social workers to help provide a framework for our coworkers to assist them in making their own decisions and to help support them in this process. It is my belief that our code of ethics offers this framework and its use in working out the problems we encounter will lead to better services for the people we are pledged to help.

Suggestions for Further Reading

Bermant, Gordon, Herbert C. Kelman, and Donald P. Warwick, eds. *The Ethics of Social Intervention*. New York: Wiley, 1978.

This book focuses on the ethics of social intervention. It contains papers presented at a foundation-sponsored conference in 1973. Topics include behavior modification; encounter groups; organizational development; community-controlled educational reform; intervention in community disputes; federally funded housing programs; and family-planning programs. The book deals with the ethical issues pertaining to these topics, presenting different perspectives so that social work students and practitioners can work through the problems and formulate their own conclusions.

Bernstein, Barton. "Malpractice, an Ogre on the Horizon." *Social Work* 23 (1978):106–111.

The possibility of social workers being sued for malpractice is dealt with, as well as the ways in which social workers can protect themselves against malpractice suits. Possible charges of malpractice include faulty diagnosis, improper treatment, a breach of confidentiality, assault and battery, sexual relationships, abandoning a client, and termination of treatment without a legitimate reason. Also discussed are damages related to monetary compensation for a wrong done to a client and behavior which reflects negatively on the social work practitioner's reputation as a professional.

Dillick, Sidney, ed. *Value Foundations of Social Work: Ethical Basis for a Human Service Profession*. Detroit, Mich.: Wayne State University, 1984.

This book contains papers presented at the Golden Jubilee of Social Work Education at Wayne State University in March of 1981. Topics include values and ethics; social work practice in health care; developing practice knowledge for black clients; ethical concerns in services to children and youth; crossroads in service delivery to the elderly; ethical issues in industrial social work; and unemployment and personal distress. Dillick concludes that the interdependence of societal values, social goals, and professional values form the basis for the ethical imperative that there be collaboration among the human service professions to achieve what society values. This provides a starting point for determining the nature of our common responsibilities, shared burdens, and the distinctive responsibilities of each of the human service professions.

- Federico, Ronald C. *The Social Welfare Institution.* Lexington, Mass.: Heath, 1984. Chapter One.

There are three value systems underlying our culture. The first is the capitalist-puritan system, which combines material and ethical values in statements regarding human nature as depraved and redeemable only by will and hard work. The second is the humanist-positivist-utopian system, which is based on the enlightenment and modern materialism. The third is the Judeo-Christian system, which is parallel to, as well as underlies, the other two systems. We need to examine these systems to determine which is more likely to preserve the values we see as important to a helping profession, and how they are concurrently affecting social welfare today.

- Green, Ronald, and G. Cox. "Social Work and Malpractice: A Converging Course." *Social Work* 23 (1978):100–104.

Owing to the rising acceptance of social work as a profession, the risk of malpractice suits against social work practitioners is also rising. This book deals with malpractice today, and how the legal system relates to current social work practice issues. Also discussed are areas in the field which are most susceptible to malpractice suits. The growing realization of the importance of a code of ethics in the regulation of practice is identified, as well as the concurrent trend toward growth in the number of malpractice suits. It is felt that these trends will help to ensure quality social work practice as well as provide social workers with a growing sense of the legal implications of their work.

- Howe, Elizabeth. "Public Professions and the Private Model of Professionalism." *Social Work* 25 (1980):179–191.

Depending upon what type of service is offered, a profession can be considered either public or private. Traditionally, professions tend to strive to develop a private model of professionalism. Social work as a profession is faced with a dilemma in terms of this, owing to the public nature of much of its work. This dilemma is discussed, and the codes of ethics of a variety of professions are compared to see how public and private models are handled. Finally, the new social work code of ethics is examined.

- Keith-Lucas, Alan. "Ethics in Social Work." *Encyclopedia of Social Work.* Washington, D.C.: NASW, 1971, pp. 324–329.

Keith-Lucas briefly defines the history and purpose of ethics in social work and then goes on to elaborate some of the major ethical problems in the field today. These are manipulation, confidentiality, advocacy, client participation, and racism. Keith-Lucas calls for a revision of the code of ethics that would be more representative of these problems. This is especially important in light of the fact that codes of ethics do not as much regulate ethics as formulate what is commonly agreed upon as ethical in a profession.

- ———. "Ethics in Social Work." *Encyclopedia of Social Work.* Washington, D.C.: NASW, 1977, pp. 350–355.

There are two kinds of situations which contain ethical implications for the social worker. The first involves a choice between a course of action that is accepted as good, moral, or correct and one which isn't. The second involves a choice between two courses of action which are both potentially good; that is the more difficult decision. The general operating principle is that the client should not be exploited for personal gain or satisfaction, whether it is financial, emotional, or a question of status and power. Some basic ethical principles are nonexploitation, nondiscrimination, the preservation of legal and constitutional rights, and the general concept of accountability. The irresolvable tensions which are inherent in "good–good" decisions are examined.

● Koerin, Beverly. "Values in Social Work Education: Implications for Baccalaureate Degree Programs." *Journal of Education for Social Work* 13 (1977):84–90.

The implications of teaching values to social work students at the baccalaureate level are discussed, and several methods for instruction are also presented. Several objectives for social work educators to strive for when teaching these values are (1) comprehension of values, disvalues, and ethical judgments; (2) appreciation of different value systems, including one's own; (3) awareness of typical professional positions with respect to values and ethics; (4) ability to interpret social work positions; and (5) ability to withstand pressures to change value positions and ethical judgments. The importance of the educator as a role model for the student is also stressed.

● Levy, Charles S. *Social Work Ethics.* New York: Human Sciences Press, 1976.

The diffusiveness of the social work profession and the diversity of its practitioners and their practices requires a systematic framework for the decisions that practitioners make when they encounter ethical issues in their practice. This book deals with why social work ethics are different from ethics in general; what it is about the profession that makes a code of ethics necessary; how the nature of social work and the context of its practice illustrate the importance of a system of ethics; how the power of the social worker can be used or misused; the importance of the anticipation of consequences as a component of ethical responsibility; how ethical social work is as planned change for a client; the appropriateness of union affiliation and participation for social workers; the various uses of a social work code of ethics depending on the professional and the context; how social work ethics could be implemented; the importance of education for the impression of ethics on the social work student; and finally, problems, prospects, and dilemmas.

● ———. "Personal vs. Professional Values: The Practitioner's Dilemma." *Clinical Social Work Journal* 4 (1976):110–120.

Professional social work practitioners may experience tension in their work due to two things: (1) they are unsure about the professional values they must abide by in their work; and (2) the very fact that they feel they have to follow professional values instead of their own personal values. Of these two sources of tension, the second causes the most concern for the practitioner. It may be that the personal values normally used to deal with people and situations conflicts with the values laid out by the profession. Ultimately, it is suggested that personal values and professional values can be integrated at the discretion of the practitioner as long as the personal values involved do not exploit or infringe on the rights of the clients.

● Lewis, Harold. *The Intellectual Base of Social Work Practice: Tools for Thought in a Helping Profession.* New York: Haworth Press, 1982.

Chapter 5—Ethics: The need for ethical imperatives is discussed. It is felt they are necessary prerequisites to achieving an important psychological influence in the service transaction. The imperative prescribes the behavior required to achieve a moral practice consistent with claimed values. The ethical dimension provides assurance to the worker that what can be done ought to be done. There is a process whereby principled behavior is achieved. It is necessary to do in order to know what it really means to act in a principled way. Formulating ethical imperatives, addressing both inductive and deductive approaches, and the importance of consistency in both personal and professional values are discussed.

Chapter 7—Values: The social worker's choice of behavior in practical situations involves judgments of principle, even when the worker does not know, but only believes, that certain consequences may follow. By assessing the consequences of value judgments, we change such judgments from imperatives to facts and contribute to a continuing dynamic between judgments and practice. The influence of structure, commands, commendations, imperatives, and norms on values are discussed. Several options are outlined that are open to a social worker faced with conflicting directives, the common denominator being that the worker believes that he or she is responsible neither for the conflict identified nor for its resolution and that the conflict is not significant or relevant to his or her practice.

- Loewenberg, Frank M. "Professional Values and Professional Ethics in Social Work Education." In Betty L. Baer and Ron Federico, eds. *Educating the Baccalaureate Social Worker*. Cambridge, Mass.: Ballinger, 1978, pp. 115–129.

    The baccalaureate social work curriculum must include content appropriate to the profession's code of ethics as well as provide the groundwork for dealing with situations of ethical conflict and ambiguity. Each part of the curriculum—the classroom, the field, peer interaction, and student–faculty contact—must be consistent in its approach to values and ethics. The importance of the teacher as role model is discussed—the greatest chance of successfully influencing the student is when the teachers are honest and authentic, make themselves available to the students outside the classroom, and risk themselves in situations similar to those in which students are expected to risk themselves. The importance of field experience is stressed; giving students the opportunity to practice the expected behaviors and to test newly learned ethics and different behavior styles, abandon previous coping mechanisms, and adopt new ones.

- Loewenberg, Frank M., and Dolgoff, Ralph. *Ethical Decisions for Social Work Practice*. Itasca, Ill.: Peacock Publishers, 1982.

    Learning to analyze the ethical problems and issues faced by social work students and practitioners in the field is covered. The material is presented in such a way that the reader will think through the ethical problems and dilemmas which occur in social work practice, to help them become more capable in coping with them. Ultimately, it is suggested that freedom and power are central issues in professional ethics and the cornerstone of most ethical problems. It is felt that the major problem is that there is contradiction between them, and the social worker's dilemma is to chose one at the expense of the other with the minimal amount of harm to the client.

- Perlman, Helen H. "Believing and Doing: Values in Social Work Education." *Social Casework* 57 (1976):381:390.

    The profession of social work is the actualization of the humanistic values held in society. This actualization is a cause for conflict because different schools of thought (i.e., the liberals and the idealists) have different ideas of how it should be done. It is felt that this type of conflict is inevitable. The goal of the social work teacher is to help the student evaluate and choose values in relation to the demands encountered in everyday life. The field of social work must continue to search for a means to resolve this conflict.

● Reamer, Frederic G. "Fundamental Ethical Issues in Social Work." *Social Service Review* 53 (1979):229–243.

Traditionally, discussions of the ethical issues in social work focus on those values basic to the profession and on building guidelines for interaction between social work practitioners and the people they deal with during their work day. A discussion of Gerwith's *Reason and Morality* and its relation to social work values and ethics is included. The origins of ethical guidelines are dealt with as well as how the principles of ethics can actually be applied in practice.

● ———. *Ethical Dilemmas in Social Service*. New York: Columbia University Press, 1982.

Current ethical dilemmas in social work are reviewed. Guidelines are developed for practitioners to use when faced with a dilemma in their work. Specific ethical questions that the practitioner frequently encounters are considered, and methods for dealing with them are examined thoroughly. The predominant concerns involved in social work practice include the question of duty to the client and the determination of who is responsible for providing aid to those in need.

● Vigilante, Joseph. "Between Values and Science: Education for the Profession during a Moral Crisis or Is Proof Truth?" *Journal of Education for Social Work* 10 (1974):107–115.

Values in social work practice are essential for proper service to the client as well as for decision making. Owing to the advent of modern science, a value conflict has emerged between humanitarianism and individualism. Individualism runs counter to the value of mutuality which is inherent in social work. Positivism cannot be used to prove that values exist. Vigilante calls for a recommitment to values in social work theory and practice, as well as for alternate research styles.

● Wilson, Suanna J. *Confidentiality in Social Work*. New York: Free Press, 1978.

This text attempts to identify the key issues relevant to confidentiality in social work practice and to offer some guidelines. Some of these issues are the confidentiality of case-record materials, release of information to others, and consumer access to record materials. Privileged communication—that is, how confidentiality is affected by the legal system—is dealt with. It is concluded that the social work profession must address these issues with greater depth, specificity, responsibility, and firmness to provide a consistency between individual social work practitioners and social work agencies in the handling of confidential material.

● Yelaja, Shankar A., ed. *Ethical Issues in Social Work*. Springfield, Ill.: Thomas, 1982.

This book contains several essays dealing with basic issues of social work ethics. Besides dealing with general issues, there are essays concerned with homosexual clients, mistreated children, older people, developmentally disabled individuals, and terminally ill patients. How these issues are related to each other are discussed, as well as the ethics surrounding the use of human beings for research and experimentation.

Appendix

THE NASW CODE OF ETHICS

I.   The Social Worker's Conduct and Comportment as a Social Worker
A.   Propriety. The social worker should maintain high standards of personal conduct in the capacity or identity as social worker.
1.   The private conduct of the social worker is a personal matter to the same degree as is any other person's, except when such conduct compromises the fulfillment of professional responsibilities.
2.   The social worker should not participate in, condone, or be associated with dishonesty, fraud, deceit, or misrepresentation.
3.   The social worker should distinguish clearly between statements and actions made as a private individual and as a representative of the social work profession or an organization or group.
B.   Competence and Professional Development. The social worker should strive to become and remain proficient in professional functions.
1.   The social worker should accept responsibility or employment only on the basis of existing competence or the intention to acquire the necessary competence.
2.   The social worker should not misrepresent professional qualifications, education, experience, or affiliations.
C.   Service. The social worker should regard as primary the service obligation of the social work profession.
1.   The social worker should retain ultimate responsibility for the quality and extent of the service that individual assumes, assigns, or performs.
2.   The social worker should act to prevent practices that are

inhumane or discriminatory against any person or group of persons.

D. Integrity. The social worker should act in accordance with the highest standards of professional integrity and impartiality.
1. The social worker should be alert to and resist the influences and pressures that interfere with the exercise of professional discretion and impartial judgement required for the performance of professional functions.
2. The social worker should not exploit professional relationships for personal gain.

E. Scholarship and Research. The social worker engaged in study and research should be guided by the conventions of scholarly inquiry.
1. The social worker engaged in research should consider carefully its possible consequences for human beings.
2. The social worker engaged in research should ascertain that the consent of participants in the research is voluntary and informed, without any implied deprivation or penalty for refusal to participate, and with due regard for participants' privacy and dignity.
3. The social worker engaged in research should protect participants from unwarranted physical or mental discomfort, distress, harm, danger, or deprivation.
4. The social worker who engages in the evaluation of services or cases should discuss them only for professional purposes and only with persons directly and professionally concerned with them.
5. Information obtained about participants in research should be treated as confidential.
6. The social worker should take credit only for work actually done in connection with scholarly and research endeavors and credit contributions made by others.

II. The Social Worker's Ethical Responsibility to Clients
F. Primacy of Clients' Interests. The social worker's primary responsibility is to clients.
1. The social worker should serve clients with devotion, loyalty, determination, and the maximum application of professional skill and competence.
2. The social worker should not exploit relationships with clients for personal advantage, or solicit the clients of one's agency for private practice.
3. The social worker should not practice, condone, facilitate or collaborate with any form of discrimination on the basis of race, color, sex, sexual orientation, age, religion, national origin, marital status, political belief, mental or

physical handicap, or any other preference or personal characteristic, condition or status.

4. The social worker should avoid relationships or commitments that conflict with the interests of clients.

5. The social worker should under no circumstances engage in sexual activities with clients.

6. The social worker should provide clients with accurate and complete information regarding the extent and nature of the services available to them.

7. The social worker should apprise clients of their risks, rights, opportunities, and obligations associated with social service to them.

8. The social worker should seek advice and counsel of colleagues and supervisors whenever such consultation is in the best interest of clients.

9. The social worker should terminate service to clients, and professional relationships with them, when such service and relationships are no longer required or no longer serve clients' needs or interests.

10. The social worker should withdraw services precipitously only under unusual circumstances, giving careful consideration to all factors in the situation and taking care to minimize possible adverse effects.

11. The social worker who anticipates the termination or interruption of service to clients should notify clients promptly and seek the transfer, referral, or continuation of service in relation to the clients' needs and preferences.

G. Rights and Prerogatives of Clients. The social worker should make every effort to foster maximum self-determination on the part of the clients.

1. When the social worker must act on behalf of a client who who has been adjudged legally incompetent, the social worker should safeguard the interests and rights of that client.

2. When another individual has been legally authorized to act in behalf of a client, the social worker should deal with that person always with the client's best interest in mind.

3. The social worker should not engage in any action that violates or diminishes the civil or legal rights of clients.

H. Confidentiality and Privacy. The social worker should respect the privacy of clients and hold in confidence all information obtained in the course of professional service.

1. The social worker should share with others confidences revealed by clients, without their consent, only for compelling professional reasons.

2. The social worker should inform clients fully about the limits of confidentiality in a given situation, the purposes for which information is obtained, and how it may be used.
3. The social worker should afford clients reasonable access to any official social work records concerning them.
4. When providing clients with access to records, the social worker should take due care to protect the confidences of others contained in those records.
5. The social worker should obtain informed consent of clients before taping, recording, or permitting third party observation of their activities.

I. Fees. When setting fees, the social worker should ensure they are fair, reasonable, considerate,and commensurate with the service performed and with due regard for the clients' ability to pay.
1. The social worker should not divide a fee or accept or give anything of value for receiving or making a referral.

III. The Social Worker's Ethical Responsibility to Colleagues
J. Respect, Fairness, and Courtesy. The social worker should treat colleagues with respect, courtesy, fairness, and good faith.
1. The social worker should cooperate with colleagues to promote professional interests and concerns.
2. The social worker should respect confidences shared by colleagues in the course of their professional relationships and transactions.
3. The social worker should create and maintain conditions of practice that facilitate ethical and competent professional performance by colleagues.
4. The social worker should treat with respect, and represent accurately and fairly, the qualifications, views, and findings of colleagues and use appropriate channels to express judgments on these matters.
5. The social worker who replaces or is replaced by a colleague in professional practice should act with consideration for the interest, character, and reputation of that colleague.
6. The social worker should not exploit a dispute between a colleague and employers to obtain a position or otherwise advance the social worker's interest.
7. The social worker should seek arbitration or mediation when conflicts with colleagues require resolution for compelling professional reasons.
8. The social worker should extend to colleagues of other professions the same respect and cooperation that is extended to social work colleagues.

9. The social worker who serves as an employer, supervisor, or mentor to colleagues should make orderly and explicit arrangements regarding the conditions of their continuing professional relationship.

10. The social worker who has the responsibility for employing and evaluating the performance of other staff members should fulfill such responsibility in a fair, considerate, and equitable manner, on the basis of clearly enunciated critera.

11. The social worker who has the responsibility for evaluating the performance of employees, supervisees, or students should share evaluations with them.

K. Dealing with Colleagues' Clients. The social worker has the responsibility to relate to the clients of colleagues with full professional consideration.

1. The social worker should not solicit the clients of colleagues.

2. The social worker should not assume professional responsibility for the clients of another agency or a colleague without appropriate communication with that agency or colleague.

3. The social worker who serves the clients of colleagues, during a temporary absence or emergency, should serve those clients with the same consideration as that afforded any client.

IV. The Social Worker's Ethical Responsibility to Employers and Employing Organizations

L. Commitments to Employing Organization. The social worker should adhere to commitments made to the employing organization.

1. The social worker should work to improve the employing agency's policies and procedures, and the efficiency and effectiveness of its services.

2. The social worker should not accept employment or arrange student field placements in an organization which is currently under public sanction by NASW for violating personnel standards, or imposing limitations on or penalties for professional actions on behalf of clients.

3. The social worker should act to prevent and eliminate discrimination in the employing organization's work assignments and in its employment policies and practices.

4. The social worker should use with scrupulous regard, and only for the purpose for which they are intended, the resources of the employing organization.

V. The Social Worker's Ethical Responsibility to the Social Work Profession

M. Maintaining the Integrity of the Profession. The social worker should uphold and advance the values, ethics, knowledge, and mission of the profession.

1. The social worker should protect and enhance the dignity and integrity of the profession and should be responsible and vigorous in discussion and criticism of the profession.

2. The social worker should take action through appropriate channels against unethical conduct by any other member of the profession.

3. The social worker should attempt to prevent the unauthorized and unqualified practice of social work.

4. The social worker should make no misrepresentation in advertising as to qualifications, competence, service, or results to be achieved.

N. Community Service. The social worker should assist the profession in making social services available to the general public.

1. The social worker should contribute time and professional expertise to activities that promote respect for the utility, the integrity, and the competence of the social work profession.

2. The social worker should support the formulation, development, enactment, and implementation of social policies of concern to the profession.

O. Development of Knowledge. The social worker should take responsibility for identifying, developing, and fully utilizing knowledge for professional practice.

1. The social worker should base practice upon recognized knowledge relevant to social work.

2. The social worker should critically examine, and keep current with, emerging knowledge relevant to social work.

3. The social worker should contribute to the knowledge base of social work and share research knowledge and practice wisdom with colleagues.

IV. The Social Worker's Ethical Responsibility to Society

P. Promoting the General Welfare. The social worker should promote the general welfare of society.

1. The social worker should act to prevent and eliminate discrimination against any person or group on the basis of race, color, sex, sexual orientation, age, religion, national origin, marital status, political belief, mental or physical handicap, or any other preference or personal characteristic, condition, or status.

2. The social worker should act to ensure that all persons have

access to the resources, services, and opportunities which they require.

3. The social worker should act to expand choice and opportunity for all persons, with special regard for disadvantaged or oppressed groups and persons.

4. The social worker should promote conditions that encourage respect for the diversity of cultures which constitute American society.

5. The social worker should provide appropriate professional services in public emergencies.

6. The social worker should advocate changes in policy and legislation to improve social conditions and to promote social justice.

7. The social worker should encourage informed participation by the public in shaping social policies and institutions.

Index